annabel langbein
Free Range in the City

From the bestselling author of The Free Range Cook

annabel langbein
Free Range in the City

Contents

introduction 6

How to use this book 10

coffee break 14

A sense of community 29

simple pleasures 42

Patio gardening 57

Eating with the seasons 66

weekend lunches 68

To market, to market 84

Pack a picnic 94

dinner in minutes 112

The urban pantry 126

The edible backyard 139

barbecues 156

Shopping with your senses 162

Develop your own free-range style 180

make-ahead meals 188

Getting organised 205

Would you like wine with that? 224

party plates 240

celebrations 266

Setting the scene 275

Creating the future 306

glossary 308

conversions 313

index 314

Welcome

People are often surprised when I say I spend more than half my life in the city. They tend to think of me as a country person, given that we film my television series *Annabel Langbein The Free Range Cook* at our little cabin on Lake Wanaka.

Wanaka is my bolt-hole, where I go to recharge my batteries and reconnect with a very simple rhythm of life, but the practicalities of modern living mean that my husband Ted and I are frequently drawn back to the rush and bustle of Auckland. That is where our work is based, where our kids went to school and where we enjoy the company of our oldest friends.

At the Wanaka cabin we grow pretty much all our own food, eat seasonally, head off on adventures to forage and fish, and connect with the seasons and our small rural community. In the city it's much harder to feel connected. When my kids were small and I was juggling the demands of bringing them up with those of a growing business, I used to end the day's work feeling exhausted. The last thing I wanted to think about was what to have for dinner, and I seldom invited people over because it felt too stressful.

In an epiphany of sorts, I decided I needed to live differently and to bring what I could of my country life to the city. After all, every moment makes up the sum of a life. So I made a conscious decision to allow time for taking a picnic lunch to the top of a hill, meeting friends after work for a barbecue at the park or beach, or having friends over for Friday drinks or a simple Sunday lunch.

I also set aside time to tend and enjoy my city garden and to visit farmers' markets at the weekends to reconnect with the rhythms of the seasons. And you know what? I was astonished at how much more in control I felt, how much more pleasure I took in small things and even the amount of money I saved. In my rush I had shopped inefficiently without checking to see what we needed, coming home with things we already had, and because I never checked use-by dates, things went off before I could use them.

In the western world we throw out an estimated 30 percent of our food. That's a huge amount of wastage – money, fuel, transportation and time – and because the bulk of the food waste goes into landfills, where it produces masses of the potent

greenhouse gas methane, it contributes dramatically to climate change. In the UK, figures show that if everyone stopped throwing away food that could have been eaten, it would have the same effect as taking one in four cars off the roads.

My television series *Annabel Langbein The Free Range Cook* struck a chord with viewers with its emphasis on getting back to the land and rediscovering forgotten domestic arts such as breadmaking and beekeeping. All around the world there is a shift towards living a simpler life. Lots of skills that have been lost by our consumer-driven generation are being revived and valued again.

Growing vegetables, keeping chickens, baking and making preserves when fruit is at its peak are simple acts that embrace a spirit of resourcefulness. Whether you're making breadcrumbs from old crusts, saving scraps for the compost bin or worm farm, freezing over-ripe bananas for smoothies or cakes, or making stock from the carcass of a roast chicken, it's about appreciating what we do have instead of constantly clamouring for more. Introducing small elements of positive change into your day doesn't have to be

a chore – in fact it's a sure-fire way to feel good about yourself. You feel so virtuous when you refuse a plastic bag at the dairy, wrap the kids' lunches in kitchen paper instead of plastic or cover your leftovers with a saucer the way your grandma did, instead of tearing off yet another sheet of plastic wrap that will never decompose.

A more resourceful and sustainable way of life doesn't need a big backyard or lots of spare time. Even if you live in an apartment or the middle of the city, with a little forethought it's easy to embrace a lifestyle that allows you to feel part of your community and environment. Daily life is more satisfying when you create small moments that take you beyond the everyday rush, when you take time in the moment to celebrate your wins, debrief on your challenges and dream for your future. And the dining table is the perfect forum for all that.

Even on days when the big picture threatens to overwhelm you, crafting good food offers a simple way to feel useful, successful and connected. There's a deep satisfaction to be found in creating a life around the kitchen table, nourishing yourself as well as others.

How to use this book

I want this book to help you easily access the kind of food you feel like eating and find recipes that match the offerings in your pantry, fridge or garden. For easy reference, the chapters are organised according to when you might want to eat the dishes – be they lunch fare, finger food or a celebration meal and so on. Of course most recipes can be used for many different occasions so these are really just a quick guide.

As a helpful cross-reference, I've put icons on each recipe showing whether it is impromptu, make-ahead, portable, freezable, vegetarian or gluten-free, and on the following pages I've listed a few of my favourites from each category.

At the back of the book is a glossary of foodie terms, substitutes, conversions and technical tips, plus a complete index based on recipe titles, key ingredients and meal types. Have a browse before you get started. Most importantly, all recipes use the fanbake (fan forced) function. If using regular bake, increase the temperature by 10°C and the cook time by 10-15 percent. That said, all ovens cook differently, so please use these times as a guide only.

You'll also find loads more information about menu planning, storecupboard essentials and kitchen know-how on my website at annabel-langbein.com. Enjoy!

 ## Menus

Deciding which dishes to put together can be the hardest part of planning and preparing a meal. To make it easy, I've created a few menu suggestions showing how you could combine some of the recipes in this book. For shopping lists, prep plans and more menu ideas, see annabel-langbein.com.

A long lunch on a cold day, page 110
Lunch with the girls, page 111
Asian flavours for unexpected guests, page 154
Retro dinner in a rush, page 155
Weekend barbecue, page 186
Seafood on the grill, page 187
Italian-inspired dinner for friends, page 238
A vegetarian feast, page 239
Christmas banquet on the lawn, page 304
Special-occasion celebration, page 305

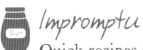

Impromptu

Quick recipes to whip up using what's in your pantry or freezer.

Snacks, starters and sides
Cheesy Rocket Scones for Beginner Bakers, 20
Quick Zucchini Fritters, 49
Fresh Herb Omelette, 50
Spiced Chickpeas and Haloumi, 58
Market Noodle Salad, 62
Tomato, Bacon and Bean Soup, 87
Lentil, Kumara and Watercress Soup, 87
Hearty Smoked Chicken Chowder, 102
Lemon Chicken Skewers with Yoghurt Sauce, 169
Purple Wheat Salad, 184
Grated Zucchini and Feta Bruschetta, 244
White Bean and Rocket Bruschetta, 244
Broccoli, Blue Cheese and Almond Tarts, 251
Tomato, Pesto and Feta Tartlets, 251
Crudité with Curry Mayo and Balsamic Oil Dips, 254
Cauliflower Broccoli Fritters with Mango Dip, 256

Main courses
Spring Prawn Salad, 52
Spiced Chickpeas and Haloumi, 58
Mushroom and Chicken Tom Yum, 61
Chicken Noodles with Asian Greens, 62
Thai-Style Tofu Fried Rice, 64
Prawn and Bean Salad, 80
Quick Smoked Chicken Pasta, 102
Smoked Chicken and Mustard Pie, 102
Beef Pho, 118
Miso-Glazed Salmon, 122
Creamy Mushroom Risotto, 128
Lime and Sesame Beef Stir-Fry, 130
Pasta with Spinach and Walnuts, 133
Pronto Pasta with Pine Nuts and Tomatoes, 133
Barbecued Chicken Chickpea Toss, 174
Help-Yourself Hot Steak Sandwiches, 179

Desserts and baking
Fresh Fruit Tartlets with Mascarpone Cream, 108
Raspberry Jam Shortbreads, 108
Roasted Plum Tarts, 108
Caramel Oranges and Kiwifruit, 146
Ginger Peach Parfait, 151

Make-Ahead

Dishes that can be prepared in advance to take the stress out of entertaining.

Snacks, starters and sides
Tomato, Bacon and Bean Soup, 87
Roasted Cauliflower and Blue Cheese Soup, 87
Hearty Smoked Chicken Chowder, 102
Scallops with Lemon Caper Butter, 164
Smoked Fish Morsels, 248
Asparagus Tarts, 251
Oysters with Kilpatrick Topping, 261

Main courses
Chicken and Prawn Gumbo, 90
Potato and Feta Picnic Pie, 96
Smoked Salmon and Egg Gratin, 99
Sensational Spinach Tart, 100
Smoked Chicken and Mustard Pie, 102
Chicken Tonnato, 140
Snapper with Black Bean Sauce, 166
Mediterranean Lamb Salad, 173
Sticky Chilli Ribs with Pineapple Salsa, 182
Spinach Ricotta Gnocchi with Walnut Butter, 192
Feta Polenta Wedges with Roast Veges, 194
Spicy Stuffed Eggplants, 196
The Ultimate Beef Fillet, 199
Tuscan Meatballs, 202
Pot-Braised Chicken with Shiitake, 206
Make-Ahead Lamb Racks, 208
Chicken, Fennel and Olive Tagine, 213
Slow-Baked Pork and Apricots, 214
Lamb and White Bean Cassoulet, 217
Coconut Tamarind Prawns, 218
Indonesian Beef Rendang, 220
Sake and Ginger Roasted Salmon, 278

Desserts and baking
Pistachio Praline Semifreddo, 229
Rocky Road Ice Cream, 152
Ginger Crème Brûlée with Mango, 226
Pistachio Praline Semifreddo, 229
Caramel Bread Puddings, 231
New York Cheesecake, 234
Raspberry Jelly Creams, 295
Triple-Chocolate Bombe, 296

 ## Portable

Great for picnics, barbecues or potluck meals – heat or assemble on-site.

Snacks, starters and sides
Cheesy Rocket Scones for Beginner Bakers, 20
Market Noodle Salad, 62
Tomato, Bacon and Bean Soup, 87
Hearty Smoked Chicken Chowder, 102
Thai Chicken Kebabs, 169
Lemon Chicken Skewers with Yoghurt Sauce, 169
Roasted Vege Orzo with Pomegranate Vinaigrette, 184
Purple Wheat Salad, 184
Asparagus Tarts, 251
Cauliflower Broccoli Fritters with Mango Dip, 256
Asian Slaw with Sake Dressing, 280

Main courses
Roast Chicken Platter with Rocket and Lemon, 77
Smoky Jo Soup, 89
Potato and Feta Picnic Pie, 96
Sensational Spinach Tart, 100
Smoked Chicken and Mustard Pie, 102
Mediterranean Lamb Salad, 173
Barbecued Chicken Chickpea Toss, 174
Grilled Lamb with Spring Burghul Salad, 174
Help-Yourself Hot Steak Sandwiches, 179
Tuscan Meatballs, 202
Chicken, Fennel and Olive Tagine, 213
Slow-Baked Pork and Apricots, 214
Lamb and White Bean Cassoulet, 217
Indonesian Beef Rendang, 220
Sake and Ginger Roasted Salmon, 278

Desserts and baking
Ginger and Apricot Biscuit Slice, 24
Chocolate Coconut Ice Slice, 31
Chocolate Chip Cookies, 32
Olive Oil Marble Cake, 35
One-Pot Chocolate and Raspberry Cupcakes, 36
Spiced Fruit Loaf, 38
Carrot Cake for a Crowd, 105
Lemon Coconut Cake, 106
Fresh Fruit Tartlets with Mascarpone Cream, 108
Strawberry Limoncello Tiramisu, 292
Festive Fruit Mince Tart, 300

 ## Freezable

Fill your freezer with these dishes, ready to thaw and reheat in a hurry.

Snacks, starters and sides
Cheesy Rocket Scones for Beginner Bakers, 20
Tomato, Bacon and Bean Soup, 87
Roasted Cauliflower and Blue Cheese Soup, 87
Lentil, Kumara and Watercress Soup, 87
Smoky Jo Soup, 89

Main courses
Malaysian Fish Laksa, 74
Chicken and Prawn Gumbo, 90
Sensational Spinach Tart, 100
Red Duck Curry, 143
Spinach Ricotta Gnocchi with Walnut Butter, 192
Tuscan Meatballs, 202
Chicken, Fennel and Olive Tagine, 213
Slow-Baked Pork and Apricots, 214
Lamb and White Bean Cassoulet, 217
Coconut Tamarind Prawns, 218
Indonesian Beef Rendang, 220

Desserts and baking
One-Pot Chocolate and Raspberry Cupcakes, 36
Gingerbread Cookies, 40
Carrot Cake for a Crowd, 105
Lemon Coconut Cake, 106
Peanut Butter and Jelly Ice Cream, 152
Coconut Ice Swirl, 152
Jaffa Ice, 152
Rocky Road Ice Cream, 152
Pistachio Praline Semifreddo, 229
Triple-Chocolate Bombe, 296
Christmas Snowballs, 302

introduction

12

Vegetarian

You don't need to be vegetarian to enjoy these meat-free recipes.

Snacks, starters and sides
Cheesy Rocket Scones for Beginner Bakers, 20
Asparagus with Poached Egg and Parmesan, 46
Egg Mayo and Olive Sandwich, 46
Tomatoes Stuffed with Chevre and Mint, 116
Baked Ricotta and Pine Nuts, 116
Grilled Veges with Sesame Sauce, 160
Mediterranean Vegetable Toss, 160
Barbecue Lemon Garlic Mushrooms, 160
Char-Grilled Red and Yellow Peppers, 160
Roasted Vege Orzo with Pomegranate Vinaigrette, 184
Purple Wheat Salad, 184
Quinoa Salad with Tomatoes and Herby Dressing, 184
Crisp Cauliflower and Cashew Salad, 223
Cucumber and Yoghurt Salad, 223
Grated Zucchini and Feta Bruschetta, 244
Bruschetta with Green Goddess Topping, 244
White Bean and Rocket Bruschetta, 244
Broccoli, Blue Cheese and Almond Tarts, 251
Asparagus Tarts, 251
Cauliflower Broccoli Fritters with Mango Dip, 256
Asian Slaw with Sake Dressing, 280
Chilli Apple and Pine Nut Salad, 280
Maple-Roasted Veges, 287
Toss of Peas and Beans, 287
Spiced Roast Potatoes, 290
Garlicky Potato Gratin, 290
Olive Oil Mash, 290

Main courses
Quick Zucchini Fritters, 49
Salad of Beets, Beans and Walnuts, 52
Spiced Chickpeas and Haloumi, 58
Lentil, Kumara and Watercress Soup, 87
Potato and Feta Picnic Pie, 96
Sensational Spinach Tart, 100
Creamy Mushroom Risotto, 128
Pasta with Spinach and Walnuts, 133
Pronto Pasta with Pine Nuts and Tomatoes, 133
Spinach Ricotta Gnocchi with Walnut Butter, 192
Feta Polenta Wedges with Roast Veges, 194
Spicy Stuffed Eggplants, 196

Gluten-Free

A listing for the gluten intolerant – always check labels for gluten traces.

Snacks, starters and sides
Tomato, Bacon and Bean Soup, 87
Roasted Cauliflower and Blue Cheese Soup, 87
Thai Chicken Kebabs, 169
Spicy Squid and Grapefruit Salad, 174
Quinoa Salad with Tomatoes and Herby Dressing, 184
Oysters with Kilpatrick Topping, 261
Mussels Florentine, 262

Main courses
Spiced Chickpeas and Haloumi, 58
Mushroom and Chicken Tom Yum, 61
Duck and Mango Salad, 72
Warm Chicken Liver Salad with Hazelnuts, 78
Prawn and Bean Salad, 80
Beef Pho, 118
Sumac and Sesame Fish with Fennel Salad, 125
Creamy Mushroom Risotto, 128
Ginger Chilli Sweet and Sour Chicken, 134
Chicken Tonnato, 140
Red Duck Curry, 143
Snapper with Black Bean Sauce, 166
Mediterranean Lamb Salad, 173
Barbecued Chicken Chickpea Toss, 174
Feta Polenta Wedges with Roast Veges, 194
Spicy Stuffed Eggplants, 196
The Ultimate Beef Fillet, 199
Make-Ahead Lamb Racks, 208
Slow-Baked Pork and Apricots, 214
Lamb and White Bean Cassoulet, 217
Coconut Tamarind Prawns, 218
Indonesian Beef Rendang, 220
Sake and Ginger Roasted Salmon, 278
Perfect Roast Lamb, 282

Desserts and baking
Peanut Butter and Jelly Ice Cream, 152
Coconut Ice Swirl, 152
Ginger Crème Brûlée with Mango, 226
Pistachio Praline Semifreddo, 229
New York Cheesecake, 234
Triple-Chocolate Bombe, 296

coffee break

Friendships blossom over coffee and cake.

In the jiggle-juggle of running jobs and families and fitting in dentists' appointments and attending committee meetings, finding time to catch up with friends can feel like yet another demand on a schedule that is already way overloaded. But we would be missing something if we didn't make time for the people who matter to us.

Some people connect through book and film clubs or craft groups, taking turns to host the event over coffee and cake or cheese and drinks. Organising a few friends to preserve or bake together is another fun way to meet up. It takes the chore out of the task at hand, everyone chips in for the costs and you divvy up what you produce.

For me, my tribe is my yoga group. For more than a decade now, five or six of us have met two or three times a week under the tutelage of a teacher whose Ursula Andress curves and smile inspire us to stretch that little bit further. Occasionally we lapse for a few weeks or even months, and then someone will rally us again, for which I (and my body) always feel hugely grateful. The fact that my friends are expecting me to turn up provides the discipline that I just can't seem to muster on my own.

We laughingly call ourselves the Chat Asanas for, as much as we work hard on our poses (actually we have never graduated beyond the primary series of ashtanga), we also chat – about the successes, laughs, labours and sadnesses of our lives. We have supported each other through infidelities, engagements, marriage breakups, job offers, redundancies, the brokering of business deals and the trials of parenting. We have shared recipes and clothes, showers, books, chutney and marmalade. We chat during particularly difficult poses, but mostly we chat afterwards, when the coffee pot goes on for a late breakfast or, sometimes, cake. It's a rhythm in my life I would hate to be without.

Liquid Gold

You can feel the goodness surging through your veins when you drink a nutritious, low-fat smoothie or juice. They are an easy way to boost your vitamin intake when you're feeling stressed or run-down – or any day for that matter, they taste so good.

Tamarillo Whizz

My favourite post-yoga morning pick-me-up is a divine fresh winter juice made by juicing together the flesh of 2 tamarillos, 2 apples and 2 oranges. Serves 1.

Dairy-Free Banana Berry Smoothie

Slice 1 banana into a blender with 1 cup frozen raspberries, 1 cup apple juice and 1 heaped tsp honey. Whizz until smooth then pour into a glass. Serves 1.

Tutti-Frutti Smoothie

Slice 1 banana into a blender with ½ cup chopped pineapple, 1 cup unsweetened low-fat yoghurt, 2 cups fresh orange juice and 2 tbsp liquid honey or maple syrup and whizz until smooth. Stir in 1 tbsp passionfruit pulp then pour into glasses. Serves 2.

Raw Energy Juice

Peel and quarter 1 raw beetroot. Top and tail 2 carrots and core 3 apples. Put through a juicer with a 2cm piece fresh ginger then pour into glasses. Serves 2.

Cheesy Rocket Scones for Beginner Bakers

This ultra-simple recipe uses fizzy soda and cream to achieve a light-as-air result. Swap the rocket for parsley or spinach if you prefer. For Sweet Orange Scones, use lemonade in place of the soda, and ½ cup sultanas or chopped dates, the finely grated zest of 1 orange and ¼ cup sugar instead of the rocket, cheese and cayenne.

Prep time	10 mins
Cook time	15-18 mins
Makes	12-16

4 cups self-raising flour, plus extra for dusting

1½ tsp baking powder

1 tsp salt

a pinch of cayenne pepper (optional)

3 handfuls (75g) rocket leaves, finely chopped

200g tasty cheese, grated

1 cup chilled cream

1 cup chilled soda water

To serve
a little butter (optional)

Preheat oven to 200°C and line a baking tray with baking paper.

In a mixing bowl combine flour, baking powder, salt and cayenne, if using. Mix in chopped rocket and cheese.

In a separate bowl or jug combine the cream and soda water. Make a well in the centre of the dry ingredients and pour in the liquid. Mix with a knife until just combined.

If making in a food processor or electric mixer, pulse together flour, baking powder, salt, cayenne, rocket and cheese to combine. Add soda and cream, pulsing 3-4 times until mixture just starts to come together.

Turn out onto a lightly floured surface and pat into a rough rectangle about 4cm thick. Cut into 12-16 pieces and place on prepared baking tray. Bake until scones are puffed and golden and they bounce back when pressed (about 15-18 minutes).

Freeze if not using the same day. When ready to use, thaw and reheat for 5 minutes in an oven preheated to 220°C.

Serve warm or at room temperature, split open and spread with a little butter, if desired. If you have any left over the next day, they are also good split in half, toasted, spread with butter and topped with sliced tomato and a little salt and pepper.

Simply Delicious Sandwiches

It's vital to use the freshest possible bread when making sandwiches – if you're not using it the same day, keep it in the freezer. When my kids were small I'd use frozen bread when I was making their lunchbox sandwiches and it would be defrosted, soft and fresh, by lunchtime.

Ham and Egg Club Sandwiches

Mash 2 hard-boiled free-range eggs finely with a fork. Mix in 2 tbsp mayonnaise (or if you prefer you can do what my mother used to do and use 2 tsp softened butter and 4 tsp milk). Add 1 tbsp chopped parsley and salt and ground black pepper to taste. Divide between 2 slices fresh sandwich bread. Top each with another slice of bread. Spread this with mayonnaise or butter, top with ham, cucumber and lettuce and season to taste. Place another slice of bread on top of each. Remove crusts and cut into 4 diagonally or into 3 fingers. Serves 2 for lunch or 4-6 for morning tea.

Cold-Smoked Salmon Sandwiches with Cress

Spread 6 slices soft wheatmeal sandwich bread on one side with butter or mayonnaise. Divide 100g cold-smoked salmon, 12-14 thin slices cucumber and 3 small handfuls cress or rocket between 3 bread slices. Season, then place bread lids on top. To remove crusts, stack sandwiches on top of one another and cut through all layers at the same time. Cut into 4 diagonally or into 3 fingers. Serves 2 for lunch or 4-6 for morning tea.

Tuna Niçoise on Turkish Flatbread

Split 1 small turkish flatbread or ciabatta loaf lengthwise and spread both sides with 4 tbsp Quick Green Sauce (see page 176) or pesto. Drain a 185g can tuna. Spread tuna on one cut side of bread and top with 2 coarsely grated hard-boiled free-range eggs and 1 roasted red pepper, peeled, deseeded and sliced (optional). Season to taste with salt and pepper. Replace top and cut into 4-6 slices. Serves 4 as a snack or 2 as lunch.

Ginger and Apricot Biscuit Slice

The ginger gives this easy, no-cook slice bite, but if you prefer you could use cinnamon or mixed spice instead. You can also replace the apricots with figs or raisins and the pistachios with walnuts or almonds. It's such a snap to make and great for picnics, school fairs and lunchboxes.

| Prep time | 20 mins +
setting time |
| Makes | about 30
pieces |

100g butter

¾ cup sweetened condensed milk

1 cup dried apricots, finely chopped

½ cup crystallised ginger, finely chopped

1 cup desiccated coconut

1 tsp ground ginger

2 tbsp lemon juice

375g plain sweet biscuits, crushed to fine crumbs

Easy Lemon Icing
50g butter

3 tbsp boiling water

1 tsp lemon juice

3½ cups icing sugar

To garnish
¼ cup crystallised ginger, chopped

2 tbsp pistachios, chopped

Line a 30cm x 24cm sponge roll tray or baking tin with baking paper.

To make the base, place butter and condensed milk in a pot and heat gently until butter melts. Remove from heat.

In a separate bowl, mix together apricots, crystallised ginger, coconut, ground ginger and lemon juice, then add crushed biscuits and stir to combine. Add butter and condensed milk mixture, stirring until well combined. Press into prepared tin and refrigerate until set (about 1 hour) before icing.

To make the Easy Lemon Icing, melt butter and mix to a smooth consistency with boiling water, lemon juice and icing sugar. Spread over base and sprinkle with chopped crystallised ginger and chopped pistachios.

When icing is set, cut into slices or squares and store in an airtight container in a cool place.

Through our children the door is open
to new friends. In their young lives there are
no boundaries of colour or creed.

A sense of community

The old bungalow we bought in the middle of the city 23 years ago was billed as a mortgagee auction, its owner up on charges for tax fraud. He had gone in full swing, ripping out walls and building new ones, extending rooflines and then – kaput – he was gone. There were no linings or ceilings. Miles of unconnected cables and wires hung loosely above our heads and there was no electricity. Fittings that had been put in, such as the bath, had been roughly pulled out by contractors who had not been paid.

It was a cold, wet winter day and my husband Ted and I stood there, wondering ever more gloomily if we had made a very, very bad decision by purchasing such a property before the actual auction. Had we paid too much? Could we ever get it right? The house was so cold and so forlorn.

Then there was a knock at the door and a bright, warm face greeted us, champagne bottle in hand. "Welcome to the neighbourhood. I'm Emerald from across the road." Suddenly we knew it would all be alright. There were people here we could laugh with and dine with and build friendships and a community with.

As the years passed and we started our family, holes were cut in hedges to allow the easy passage of small feet; neighbourhood kids would come over after school to bake or pick flowers from the garden. Our street was filled with laughing children, great cooks and prolific gardens. Friendships were built over casual neighbourly lunches and dinners, fruits and vegetables were swapped and in times of need the neighbourhood would rally with soup and support.

Kids make it easy to build neighbourhood friendships because they are always out and about, looking for playmates. In their young lives there are no boundaries of colour or religion or creed – their offer of friendship is fearless. Through them the door is open for us to make new friends.

Now the tribe of kids we knew have all grown up and flown the nest. People have moved on, the street has become increasingly taken over by businesses, and there are fewer and fewer people in the neighbourhood whom we know. But a jar of jam, a plate of home-made biscuits or a pot of soup are ready, waiting for when the next door opens.

Chocolate Coconut Ice Slice

This recipe is so simple my two kids have been making variations of it ever since they could reach the kitchen bench. The base is a stir-together mixture using crushed biscuits and the icing can be varied to suit your tastes – sometimes I leave out the cocoa and make pink icing like regular coconut ice.

Prep time   15 mins + setting time

Makes   about 30 pieces

150g melted butter

1 cup sweetened condensed milk

2 tbsp golden syrup

1½ cups desiccated coconut

½ cup cocoa

¾ cup icing sugar

2 tsp vanilla extract

375g plain, sweet biscuits, crushed to coarse crumbs

Chocolate Coconut Icing
200g dark chocolate

40g butter

1½ cups icing sugar

3 tbsp boiling water

1½ cups desiccated coconut

Line a 30cm x 24cm sponge roll tray or baking tin with baking paper.

To make the base, place butter, condensed milk and golden syrup in a pot or microwave-proof bowl large enough to hold the entire mixture. Heat gently on stovetop or in the microwave until the butter melts. Remove from heat. Mix together coconut, cocoa, icing sugar and vanilla. Stir into butter and condensed milk mixture then stir in biscuit crumbs. Press into prepared tin and refrigerate until set (about 1 hour) before icing.

To make the Chocolate Coconut Icing, break chocolate into squares and melt with butter in a double boiler or microwave (microwave on medium for 30-second bursts for about 1½ minutes, stirring between each burst, until runny and smooth). Mix to a smooth consistency with icing sugar and boiling water. Stir through coconut and spread over base. Refrigerate until set.

When icing is set, cut into slices or squares and store in an airtight container in a cool place.

Chocolate Chip Cookies

The trick to these buttery cookies is chopping the chocolate roughly so it melts into luscious nuggets when they are baked. This generous double recipe makes about 70 cookies, so you can give half away to a friend or stash them for another day. It's the sweetened condensed milk that makes them so crispy.

Prep time	10 mins
	+ chilling
Cook time	15 mins
Makes	about 70

500g butter, softened

1 cup sugar

½ cup sweetened condensed milk

½ tsp vanilla extract

4½ cups flour

4 tsp baking powder

500g dark chocolate, chopped into chunks

Preheat oven to 160°C and line 3 oven trays with baking paper.

Beat butter and sugar until creamy. Beat in condensed milk and vanilla. Stir in flour, baking powder and chopped chocolate. Don't overmix. Chill for 15 minutes until the mixture is firm enough to shape and roll.

Roll into walnut-sized balls and place on cold oven trays, allowing room in between for spreading. Flatten firmly onto trays with the palm of your hand and flatten again with the tines of a fork to make thin, crisp biscuits. Bake until lightly golden (about 15 minutes). Cool then remove from trays and store in an airtight container.

Just the smell
of baking makes
a house feel
like a home.

Olive Oil Marble Cake

I discovered this rustic tea cake in Umbria years ago and it has been a staple ever since. I love the way you can whizz the whole thing up in a food processor or mixer to produce a moist cake that keeps fresh for days. Don't be tempted to leave out the rum – the alcohol evaporates on cooking, adds flavour and helps keep the cake tender.

Prep time — 15 mins
Cook time — 55-60 mins
Makes — 1 large cake

4 eggs

1½ cups sugar

½ cup milk

¾ cup extra light olive oil

2¼ cups flour

3 tsp baking powder

finely grated zest of 2 lemons

1 tsp vanilla extract

½ tsp ground cloves

1 tsp ground allspice

4 tbsp rum

1 tbsp cocoa, sifted

Preheat oven to 150°C. Grease a 25-26cm round springform cake tin and line with baking paper.

Place eggs and sugar in a food processor or electric mixer and whizz until light and fluffy. Add milk and oil and whizz again to combine. Add flour, baking powder, lemon zest, vanilla, cloves, allspice and just 3 tbsp of the rum and pulse 4-5 times until smooth. Mixture is quite runny.

Pour all but ¾ cup of the batter into the prepared cake tin (don't be tempted to save more). Mix sifted cocoa and remaining 1 tbsp rum together and then stir into the reserved ¾ cup of cake mixture until well combined. Drizzle this mixture over the top of the cake to create the marbling effect.

Bake until a skewer inserted into the centre of the cake comes out clean (about 55-60 minutes). Allow cake to cool in the tin for 10-15 minutes before turning out onto a cake rack. Store in an airtight container for up to a week.

One-Pot Chocolate and Raspberry Cupcakes

If I'm going to make cupcakes I like to make a lot, so this is a double recipe. Not only do the iced cupcakes freeze well, but the raw batter and icing both keep in the fridge for up to a week so you can cook a fresh batch every morning.

Prep time	25 mins
	+ standing
Cook time	20 mins
Makes	24

120g butter, in small dice

½ cup neutral oil

1 cup water

100g dark chocolate, chopped

½ cup cocoa, sifted

1½ cups caster sugar

2 eggs

1 tsp vanilla extract

1½ tsp baking powder

1 tsp baking soda

1 cup yoghurt or buttermilk

2 cups flour

¾ cup raspberries

In The Pink Frosting
120g butter

200g cream cheese

2 tbsp blackcurrant cordial

1 tsp vanilla extract

5-6 drops red food colouring

5 cups icing sugar, sifted

candy sprinkles

Preheat oven to 180°C. Line 24 muffin pans with paper cases.

Place butter, oil, water and chocolate in a medium-large pot and melt over medium heat. Turn off heat and whisk in cocoa and caster sugar, making sure there are no lumps of cocoa. Whisk in eggs and vanilla.

Mix baking powder and baking soda into yoghurt or buttermilk then add to chocolate mixture with flour, whisking until evenly combined to a smooth batter. Stand for at least 10 minutes before cooking.

Spoon mixture into paper cases, using about 3 tbsp per cupcake to ¾ fill each case. Push 2-3 raspberries into each (if berries are frozen, stand cupcakes a further 10 minutes before cooking).

Bake cupcakes until they are risen and the tops bounce back when gently pressed (about 20 minutes). Stand 5 minutes before lifting out of tins. Ice when cold.

To make In The Pink Frosting, bring butter and cream cheese to room temperature, then beat together with blackcurrant cordial, vanilla and colouring until creamy smooth. Add icing sugar and beat until smooth. Chill for 10 minutes. At this point the mixture should hold its texture when you spoon it. If it is too thin, add a little more icing sugar. Put into a piping bag and pipe onto cooled cupcakes. Garnish with candy sprinkles.

Spiced Fruit Loaf

The recipe for this dense fruit loaf originally belonged to my nan, who used to bake it in her coal range. It's one of those recipes that seems to improve after a day or two, a bit like gingerbread. It's lovely sliced and buttered and enjoyed with a cup of tea.

Prep time	10 mins
	+ cooling
Cook time	1 hour
Makes	1 loaf

1 cup sugar

50g butter

1 cup sultanas

1 cup dates

1 tbsp golden syrup

1¼ cups water

1 tsp mixed spice

1 tsp ground ginger

½ cup walnuts, chopped

½ tsp vanilla extract

¼ tsp salt

2 cups flour

1 tsp baking soda

1 tsp baking powder

Preheat oven to 170°C. Grease a 23cm x 14cm loaf tin and line with baking paper.

Place sugar, butter, sultanas, dates, golden syrup and water in a large pot. Bring to a boil and simmer for 5 minutes. Remove from heat and leave to cool for 10 minutes.

Stir mixed spice, ginger, walnuts, vanilla and salt into the date mixture. Add flour, baking soda and baking powder and mix to combine. Pour into prepared loaf tin and bake 1 hour or until a skewer inserted in the centre comes out clean. Leave to cool in tin for 15 minutes before turning out onto a wire rack.

Gingerbread Cookies

This is a great recipe, neither too sweet nor too spicy. You can make the dough in bulk and store it tightly covered in the fridge for up to a week, or freeze it until you're ready to cook it. Have fun playing around with spices – try omitting the allspice and ginger and increasing the cinnamon to 1 tbsp.

Prep time	15 mins
Cook time	15 mins
Makes	48 small or
	24 big shapes

150g butter, softened

¼ packed cup
soft brown sugar

3 tbsp golden syrup

1 tsp baking soda

1½ tsp boiling water

2¼ cups flour

3 tsp ground ginger

1 tsp cinnamon

1 tsp allspice

candy sprinkles (optional)

Royal Icing
1 egg white

2 cups icing sugar, sifted,
plus a little extra for dusting

Preheat oven to 150°C. Line 2-3 oven trays with baking paper.

Beat together butter, sugar and golden syrup until pale and creamy. Mix baking soda with boiling water and add to butter mixture with flour, ginger, cinnamon and allspice. Stir to combine into a pliable dough. If not using at once, cover and chill for up to a week or freeze until needed.

Divide dough into 3 pieces and sprinkle each piece lightly with flour for easier handling. Roll out each piece thinly to ½cm thickness, using a little flour to dust the roller (avoid using too much flour when you roll the dough as this dries out the mixture). If using candy sprinkles, scatter over rolled dough and lightly roll again to press in.

Cut dough into shapes. Carefully transfer to prepared baking trays, allowing a little space between biscuits for spreading. Form unused dough into a ball and roll and cut again.

Bake until just starting to colour (about 15 minutes). Remove from oven and allow to cool on the trays; they will harden as they cool. Store in an airtight container until ready to ice.

Ice biscuits with Royal Icing up to 5 days before serving (they will soften just a little once they have been iced). To make Royal Icing, gently beat the egg white until slightly airy. Add sifted icing sugar and beat for 10 minutes. Spoon into a piping bag and pipe decorations onto cookies. Allow to set. If desired, dust cookies lightly with icing sugar before serving.

With a few basic ingredients it's so easy to create the kind of kitchen magic that inspires a lifelong love of cooking.

simple pleasures

In a busy life, time to yourself
is the ultimate indulgence.

Having the house to myself, with no one else to think about, always feels like a bit of a luxury. If I fancy a soak in the bath with a bowl of cereal and hot milk at midnight, well I can. There is no hour (or location for that matter – the sofa often looks pretty good) that can be deemed inappropriate for eating.

But after a couple of days of lazily indulging myself, I'm ready for some real food and some company to cook for. The trouble is, when you're home alone, it's horribly easy to fall into a rut of eating snacks as meals, consuming loads of processed, packaged foods and having a speed-dial relationship with your favourite neighbourhood take-out.

My strategy is to have really delicious things on hand in the fridge and pantry. Because one person can only get through so much food in a day, I look for things that won't go off quickly and will add pizzazz to simple dishes: cheeses, olives, fresh pestos and dressings and quality artisan-style dips and spreads, along with fresh salad vegetables, fruit and, of course, ever-useful eggs.

My favourite "instant" food is a bowl of rice (from the freezer) with poached eggs, spinach and parmesan. In the three or four minutes it takes to poach the eggs, the rice heats in the microwave, the spinach is wilted and the cheese grated. Or serve steamed broccoli over warmed hummus with toasted sesame seeds. Another good storecupboard combo is a can of white beans tossed with a can of tuna, lemon-garlic olive oil, red peppers, tomatoes and rocket.

This kind of food is less about cooking and more about selecting good ingredients and assembling them in tasty, nutritious ways. That way you can assuage the craving for a quick meal and at the same time make some savings in your purse and probably your waistline.

Easy Ideas for Eggs

Eggs are one of my desert-island foods. When I want a nourishing lunch or light supper in a hurry, they tick all the boxes. Super-fresh eggs are best for poaching, but adding 1 tsp vinegar to the water helps hold older eggs together. I love the deep orange colour the yolks become when the hens have been pecking on fresh greens.

Asparagus with Poached Egg and Parmesan

Trim a handful of asparagus spears, plunge into a pot of lightly salted boiling water and cook 3 minutes. Lift out asparagus with tongs and transfer to a plate. Return pot to a low heat and when water is gently simmering, break in a very fresh free-range egg and cook until soft-poached (about 3 minutes). Serve asparagus topped with egg, parmesan shavings, a drizzle of boutique extra virgin olive oil and coarsely ground black pepper. Serves 1.

Egg Mayo and Olive Sandwich

Mash a hard-boiled free-range egg finely with a fork. Mix in 1 tbsp mayonnaise (or use 1 tsp softened butter and 2 tsp milk). Add 1 tsp finely chopped chives or parsley and salt and ground black pepper to taste. Spread onto a slice of fresh wholegrain sandwich bread, top with 4 pitted, chopped kalamata olives and a small handful of salad greens. Slather another slice of bread with mayonnaise or aioli and place on top of the sandwich. Serves 1.

Soft-Poached Egg on Mushrooms

Heat 1 tbsp butter in a pot and cook 150g small white button mushrooms, quartered, over medium-high heat, stirring frequently until lightly browned (about 2-3 minutes). Add 1 crushed clove garlic and the finely grated zest of ½ a lemon and cook 1 minute more. Mix ½ cup chicken stock with 1 tsp cornflour and 1 tsp porcini or dried mushroom powder (optional) and stir into the mushrooms. Simmer over low heat for 2 minutes. Break a very fresh free-range egg into gently simmering, lightly salted water and cook until soft-poached (about 3 minutes). Mix 1 tsp lemon juice and 1 tsp chopped parsley into the mushrooms and season to taste with salt and pepper. Spoon onto a plate and top with the poached egg. Serves 1. The mushrooms are also great on toast or bruschetta.

Quick Zucchini Fritters

Making this batter really thick means you end up with substantial yet light fritters. To cook these for friends or family simply double or quadruple the recipe. If you prefer corn and feta fritters, simply replace the zucchini with a cup of corn kernels. You can also use blue cheese or parmesan instead of the feta.

Prep time	10 mins
Cook time	5-7 mins
Serves	1

1 medium zucchini

1 egg

3 tbsp self-raising flour

30g feta, crumbled

1 tbsp finely chopped spring onion or chives

1 small clove garlic, crushed

1 tbsp finely chopped mint

1 tsp lemon juice

a pinch of chilli flakes

salt and ground black pepper

½ tbsp butter

To serve
fresh salad garnish

lemon wedges

Coarsely grate zucchini onto a clean teatowel, pull up the sides of the teatowel and twist and squeeze tightly over the sink to remove as much liquid as possible.

Mix egg and flour to make a very thick, smooth batter. Add grated zucchini, feta, spring onion or chives, garlic, mint, lemon juice, chilli flakes and salt and pepper to taste and stir well.

Melt butter in a heavy-based frypan then tip the melted butter into the batter and stir until evenly combined. Use this same pan without washing to cook fritters. Spoon mixture into hot pan, using about 2 tbsp for each fritter to make 4 medium-sized fritters. Flatten slightly.

Cook fritters over medium heat for 2-3 minutes on each side or until mixture is fully cooked through to the centre. Serve with salad leaves and lemon wedges.

Fresh Herb Omelette

This light, tender omelette filled with crispy bacon, wilted greens and two kinds of cheese is exactly the kind of meal I crave when I'm at home alone and feeling like some quick comfort food. Serve it with a slice of wholegrain bread and you've got all your food groups covered. Leave the bacon out for a vegetarian version.

Prep time	5 mins
Cook time	5 mins
Serves	1

3 free-range eggs

½ tsp salt

ground black pepper

1 tbsp feta, crumbled

1 tsp butter

1 rasher streaky bacon, finely diced (optional)

2 handfuls (50g) watercress or baby spinach

1 tbsp mozzarella, grated

1 tbsp finely chopped chervil or parsley leaves

To serve
juice of ½ lemon

Lightly whisk eggs, season with salt and pepper and mix in feta.

Heat butter in a frypan and sizzle bacon, if using, until starting to crisp. Add half the watercress or spinach and stir over medium heat until wilted (about 30 seconds).

Pour egg mixture into pan on top of the bacon and greens, tilting to spread evenly. Loosen a couple of times with a knife or spatula at the start of cooking to allow raw egg to run into the base of the pan.

As the mixture sets, sprinkle with mozzarella and top with the rest of the greens and the chervil or parsley. Cook until the egg is almost set (about another 1 minute), then fold in half, drizzle with lemon juice and serve.

Sensational Salads

My favourite summer meal when I'm cooking for one is a leafy green salad tossed with a few chopped vegetables, a light dressing and whatever protein is handy in the fridge. To feed more people, simply double or quadruple the ingredients.

Salad of Beets, Beans and Walnuts

Peel 2 medium beetroots, halve and cut each half into 5-6 wedges. Place in a pot with 2 tsp brown sugar, 1 tbsp balsamic vinegar, ½ cup water, 1 tbsp olive oil and a little salt and pepper. Cover and cook over medium heat until almost tender (about 12-15 minutes). Remove lid and continue to cook until liquid has all but evaporated, watching carefully to ensure it does not burn. Leave to cool. Toss cooled beetroot with 2 handfuls salad greens or baby beetroot leaves, ½ cup toasted walnuts or almonds and ¼ cup peeled broad beans or edamame. Pile onto a serving plate, top with 30g crumbled or sliced goat cheese or feta, drizzle with a little boutique extra virgin olive oil and finish with salt and pepper to taste. Serves 1 as a meal or 2 as a starter.

Spring Prawn Salad

Mix 150g large raw prawn tails with ½ tsp sesame oil, 1 tsp grated fresh ginger, the finely grated zest of ¼ lime and salt and pepper. Cover and stand 15 minutes or chill up to 4 hours. Heat 2 tsp neutral oil in a heavy-based frypan and fry prawns over high heat until opaque (1-2 minutes each side). Remove from heat and stir in 2 tsp lime juice, 1 tsp soy sauce and 1 tbsp toasted sesame seeds. Thinly slice the crunchy white ends of ½ head bok choy and place in a bowl with a generous handful of baby spinach or rocket. Add prawns and their pan liquids and toss to serve. Serves 1.

Summer Salad with Hot-Smoked Salmon

Place a big handful of baby cos lettuce leaves on a plate and top with 50g hot-smoked salmon, broken into large flakes. Toss with the juice of ½ a lemon and top with 1 halved hard-boiled free-range egg, the thinly sliced white of 1 spring onion, 1 thinly sliced celery stalk and fine strands of lemon zest. Season with salt and pepper and drizzle with aioli, mayonnaise or Basic Vinaigrette (see page 173). Serves 1.

There's something very empowering about
planting seeds and nourishing them to harvest,
even if it's just a tiny pot of herbs.

Patio gardening

Recently I found myself on my friend Georgie's tiny terrace in Paris. She has often talked about her garden but, given she lives seven floors up in an apartment with only a narrow balcony, I had not imagined an actual garden. But here I was, immersed in nature and colour and scent, worlds away from pavements and cars and the jangle of the city.

Every scrap of space was filled with planter boxes packed with healthy plants: blowsy dahlias, figs, limes, roses and fragrant herbs, all tangled together in lush profusion. That small space delivered so much pleasure as well as a sense of connection to the rhythms of nature and the seasons.

If you live in an apartment you may not even have a balcony, but just a couple of planter pots or a windowsill box of herbs and vegetables will provide lashings of satisfaction as well as making everything you cook taste so much better.

Adding fresh herbs makes food taste vivid and fresh. With their dense, strong flavours, woody herbs add depth as well as freshness to any sauce, soup, stew or risotto. Rosemary, thyme, sage, oregano and marjoram can sit in little pots on the windowsill for years. They tolerate drought and neglect more than most plants, provided they get sun. Mint and chives like it damp and shady – you might want to pot them in the bathroom!

Seasonal soft herbs such as parsley, basil, coriander, chervil and dill can be planted densely for regular snipping and add a bright, clean note to the plate. I always add soft herbs at the end of cooking to preserve their fresh tastes.

Growing salad greens or any kind of micro-greens is worthwhile. They take only a few weeks when the weather is warm and they'll even grow on a windowsill in winter if you put a little clear cover over the top like a mini glasshouse to get them started. Plant a whole packet of seeds into a 20-30cm pot and sow a new potful every week or so. In three to six weeks you'll be rewarded with a forest of tiny green seedlings. For micro-greens, snip these off when they reach about 2-3cm. For salad leaves, wait another week or two and cut them when they reach 6-15cm. As long as you leave about 5mm they'll grow back again and you can get a succession of three or four harvests.

For more gardening advice see annabel-langbein.com

Spiced Chickpeas and Haloumi

I always make enough of this for two or three servings so I can have some the next day – if anything, it tastes even better when the flavours have been allowed to develop. It's also great as a side dish with grilled lamb, chicken or beef. Use cypriot-style haloumi if possible as it holds its shape better when cooked.

Prep time 5 mins
Cook time 10 mins
Serves 2-3 as a meal or 4-6 as a side

2 tbsp neutral oil

2 cloves garlic, crushed

2 tsp ground cumin

½ tsp chilli flakes

½ tsp fennel seeds (optional)

400g chickpeas, rinsed and drained

200g cypriot-style haloumi or firm paneer, cut into 1-2cm chunks

1 tbsp tomato paste

1 tsp brown sugar

400g can cherry tomatoes in juice

salt and ground black pepper

5-6 handfuls (130-150g) baby spinach or roughly chopped spinach leaves

2 tbsp greek yoghurt

In a medium pot, heat oil and sizzle garlic, cumin, chilli and fennel seeds, if using, for a few seconds. Add chickpeas and haloumi or paneer and cook 2-3 minutes to infuse spice flavours.

Stir in tomato paste, then add sugar and canned tomatoes in their juice. Season with salt and pepper to taste and simmer gently for 3-5 minutes.

Add spinach, cover with a lid and cook until spinach has wilted (about 2 minutes). Stir in yoghurt just before serving, or serve it on the side as a garnish.

With a global pantry at your fingertips you can travel the world without leaving home.

Mushroom and Chicken Tom Yum

One-pot, one-bowl meals are ideal when you're eating on your own. For one thing, there are fewer dishes to deal with. This zingy soup is equally good with prawns and can be extended into a more substantial meal by adding a little extra stock and two heads of chopped bok choy and serving in deep bowls over cooked noodles.

Prep time	10 mins
Cook time	6 mins
Serves	2

1 litre well-flavoured
chicken stock

12 button mushrooms,
quartered

2 tomatoes, cored and diced

1 tsp tomato paste

½ tsp dried chilli flakes,
or more to taste

finely grated zest of 1 lime

2 tbsp fish sauce

2 kaffir lime leaves
or zest of 1 lime

1 skinless single chicken
breast, very thinly sliced

4 tbsp fresh lime juice,
or more to taste

salt and ground black pepper

To serve
4 tbsp chopped coriander
or mint leaves

Place chicken stock, mushrooms, tomatoes, tomato paste, chilli flakes, lime zest, fish sauce and lime leaves or zest in a medium-sized pot. Simmer for 5 minutes.

Just before serving, add sliced chicken breast and simmer until it has turned white and is cooked through (about 1 minute).

Mix in lime juice and adjust seasoning, adding salt and pepper or more lime juice as needed. Remove kaffir lime leaves, if using. To serve, ladle soup into a bowl and scatter coriander or mint leaves over the top. The remainder can be reheated for lunch or dinner the next day or delivered to a friend who has the flu – it's brilliant for blasting away the bugs.

Noodle Love

There's something wonderfully reassuring about settling down on the sofa with a bowl of flavoursome noodles. These recipes make extra in case a friend pops in, or can easily be doubled if you want to feed more.

Salmon Noodle Bowl

Slice 250-300g boneless, skinless salmon into finger-wide strips and stir into a marinade of 1 tsp sesame oil, 1 finely sliced spring onion, 2 tbsp grated fresh ginger, 1 tsp soft brown sugar and ¼ cup light soy sauce. Chill 15 minutes or up to 4 hours. Meanwhile, cook 270-300g dried udon or soba noodles according to packet instructions, adding about 70g snow peas in the last 30 seconds. Drain at once and refresh in cold water. Remove salmon from marinade, heat 2 tbsp neutral oil in a wok and cook salmon 2 minutes without turning. Pile noodles and snow peas on top and add marinade and 2 tbsp water. Cover and cook over medium-low heat for 3 minutes without stirring. Tip into a serving bowl and sprinkle with 2 tsp black sesame seeds. Serves 2.

Market Noodle Salad

To make the dressing, whizz 1 clove garlic, 1 tbsp grated fresh ginger, 1 tbsp soy sauce, 1 tbsp thai sweet chilli sauce, 2 tsp fish sauce, 1 tbsp peanut butter, 1 chopped spring onion, a handful of coriander leaves and 4 tbsp water in a food processor until semi-smooth. Cook 350-400g dried udon or soba noodles according to packet instructions. Place drained noodles in a bowl with dressing, ¼ cup roasted peanuts, 1 finely chopped spring onion, 2 tbsp chopped coriander or mint leaves, ¼ cucumber cut in small batons and ½ diced red or green pepper. Toss to combine and serve at room temperature. Serves 4. Delicious with Thai Chicken Kebabs (see page 169).

Chicken Noodles with Asian Greens

Gently simmer 4 cups chicken stock with 2 tbsp grated fresh ginger, 1 crushed clove garlic, 2 tsp sesame oil, 1 tbsp fish sauce, ½ tsp chilli flakes and 1 kaffir lime leaf or the finely grated zest of 1 lime for 8-10 minutes. Thinly slice 300-400g skinless, boneless chicken thighs, add to pan and simmer gently for 5 minutes. Meanwhile, cook 180-200g dried udon noodles in a separate pot according to packet instructions. Peel and halve lengthwise 4-5 stalks gai lan or choy sum or cut 1 small head broccoli into florets and add to the noodles in the last 3 minutes of cooking. Drain and divide between warmed bowls. Add 2 thinly sliced spring onions. Top with soup, squeeze over the juice of ½ a lemon and sprinkle with 2 tbsp black sesame seeds. Serves 2.

Thai-Style Tofu Fried Rice

Whenever we have rice I cook extra so there's some in the fridge or freezer for another day. I'll fry it up with whatever vegetables are at hand, but this Asian tofu combination is one of my favourites. If I'm really hungry I'll top it with a fried egg. If you're vegetarian, use tamari instead of fish sauce.

Prep time	10 mins
	+ marinating
Cook time	8 mins
Serves	1-2

300g tofu, cut into 1-2cm dice

3 tbsp soy sauce

2 tbsp neutral oil

2 cloves garlic, crushed

1 tbsp grated fresh ginger

1 green pepper, cored, deseeded and finely diced

2 spring onions, thinly sliced

½ green chilli, deseeded and finely sliced (optional)

2 free-range eggs

2 tsp fish sauce

3 cups cooked rice

2 handfuls bean sprouts or finely chopped bok choy stalks or cabbage

2 tbsp toasted peanuts

2 tbsp chopped coriander

To serve
thai sweet chilli sauce

lime wedges

Place tofu in a bowl with 1 tbsp soy sauce and stir through to coat evenly. Set aside to marinate for at least 10 minutes or up to 4 hours.

When ready to serve, heat oil in a heavy-based frypan and fry tofu over high heat until lightly browned (about 2 minutes). Add garlic, ginger, green pepper, spring onions and chilli, if using, and sizzle for 30 seconds, stirring constantly.

Lightly whisk eggs and fish sauce together in a bowl and add to pan, stirring until eggs are set in curds. Add rice, bean sprouts or bok choy or cabbage and remaining 2 tbsp soy sauce and cook, stirring now and then, until heated through (about 5 minutes).

Add peanuts and coriander. Pile into a bowl or plate, drizzle with thai sweet chilli sauce to taste and serve with lime wedges to squeeze over the top. Makes enough for today with some left over for tomorrow.

Eating with the seasons

If you live in the city it's much harder to be connected with the rhythms of nature than when you live in the country. At the supermarket you can get pretty much any item of produce in year-round supply, so you don't always know when or whether something is actually in season.

Sourcing fresh fruit and vegetables from our own backyard gardens, farmers' markets and weekly produce boxes changes the way we eat – whatever is in season is what there is to cook, so we build our meals around it.

In the ebb and flow of the farmers' market or your own garden you can feel and taste the shift of the seasons. A pleasing spirit of resourcefulness and creativity comes to bear when your cooking is seasonally driven.

In spring, palates jaded from a winter of soups and stews are tempted by the first strawberries, early rhubarb, waxy new potatoes and soft new-season greens such as vibrant broad beans and snow peas and the tender tips of asparagus.

Summer and autumn spoil us for choice with an abundance of sun-ripened flavours. The rich, heady fragrance of white peaches and melons and the sweet scent of lavender and herbs spell summer, sun and flavour.

In the autumn, a riot of harvests competes for our attention: pungent, earthy tomatoes, onions, eggplants, zucchini, peppers, chillies, corn and pumpkins, as well as all manner of stone and pip fruit and the second flush of berries. There is so much choice.

But in winter when there are no tomatoes, zucchini or peppers, we turn to roasted root vegetables, rich vegetable soups, tagines, curries, braises and cheesy gratins to take advantage of the abundance of winter root crops as well as hardy above-ground types such as leeks, celery, brassicas and winter greens. Winter's arrival sees only the hardiest of growers out in the cold at the farmers' markets with their harvests of stored potatoes, pumpkins, onions, garlic, apples and pears, and freshly dug celeriac, parsnips, carrots and beets.

Experiencing the natural rhythm of the seasons allows us to celebrate and enjoy each season's unique harvests, knowing that there is a time and a place for everything in the cycles of nature.

For a seasonal growing guide see annabel-langbein.com

weekend lunches

While away the day over a long, lazy lunch.

Saturday mornings are almost the best part of living in a city. There's a wonderful sense of anticipation when you wake up with 48 free hours ahead of you – farmers' markets to visit, friends to laugh with over lengthy lunches, big walks, no deadlines. It's these aimless, indulgent days that lasting memories are made of.

In our house the weekend usually starts with the same pleasing routine: a wander down to our favourite coffee shop to linger over the paper with a really good coffee and a tartine (french bread with butter and jam), then a stroll to the local farmers' markets to be wowed by the week's offerings. We lug our goodies home and turn them into a fabulous lunch, piling everything onto the table and greedily tucking in.

But Sunday is when I like to hang out over a lazy lunch with my nearest and dearest. It's probably my favourite way to while away an afternoon and catch up properly with people I don't get to spend enough time with during the busy working week.

If you want to, you can get creative, experiment and take your time. But the principle of lunch is simple, and that's what makes it so good. There's none of the multi-course dinner menu thing happening and, unlike dinner, when people have to rush home to bed so they can get up the next morning, lunch is relaxed. There's no sense of expectation or culinary hype – everyone just wants to enjoy the afternoon relaxing over a simple meal.

If it's blowing a gale outside, I'll simmer a pot of soup on the stove and pop a cake in the oven. If the sun is shining, a flavoursome salad is a tempting offering. When the weather holds we will head outside for a walk between courses, returning home to enjoy coffee and dessert. And when it's really good, lunch can last until dinnertime.

Duck and Mango Salad

Duck marries well with Asian flavours, including this Ginger Sesame Dressing. The dressing keeps well in the fridge and is great over any Asian salad. You could roast a whole duck yourself, but I usually save time by buying one ready-roasted from my local Asian supermarket – it makes this salad so easy.

Prep time   20 mins
Serves   8

1 roasted duck

100g snow peas

2 large, ripe mangos

3 just-ripe avocados

1 red pepper, deseeded

2 spring onions or ¼ red onion

150-200g baby spinach leaves
or mixed salad leaves

½ cup chopped mint
or coriander leaves

2 handfuls mung bean sprouts
(optional)

Ginger Sesame Dressing
¼ cup lime or lemon juice

2 tsp fish sauce

1 tsp soft brown sugar

1 tsp sesame oil

1 tsp grated fresh ginger

1 tbsp rice vinegar

1 tbsp soy sauce or tamari

1 small red chilli, deseeded
and finely chopped

salt and ground black pepper

To make Ginger Sesame Dressing, shake together in a small jar the lime or lemon juice, fish sauce, brown sugar, sesame oil, ginger, rice vinegar, soy sauce or tamari, chilli, salt and pepper. Ginger Sesame Dressing keeps in the fridge for up to a week.

Strip the duck from the bones, discarding skin and fat and reserving bones to make stock if desired. Place duck in a bowl with half the Ginger Sesame Dressing and toss to coat.

Pour boiling water over the snow peas, drain immediately then cover with cold water and drain again. Peel, destone and chop mangos and avocados. Finely slice red pepper and spring onions or red onion.

Place spinach or salad leaves on a serving platter and add snow peas, mango, avocado, red pepper, spring onions or red onion, mint or coriander and mung bean sprouts, if using. Add duck and its dressing, toss with remaining dressing and serve at once.

Malaysian Fish Laksa

Using store-bought laksa paste makes authentic-tasting laksa a snap. If you can't find any, use thai green curry paste – the flavour will be different but still good. You could add other seafood, such as crabmeat and prawns, to make Seafood Laksa, or use finely sliced chicken breast and chicken stock to make Chicken Laksa.

Prep time	10 mins
Cook time	15 mins
Serves	4

400g dried udon noodles

300g skinless, boneless white fish fillets, cut into 2cm pieces

salt and ground black pepper

Laksa Base
2 tbsp neutral oil

1 tbsp grated fresh ginger

2 cloves garlic, crushed

2-3 tbsp laksa paste

finely grated zest of 1 lime

1 litre fish stock

1 cup coconut cream

1 tsp soft brown sugar

2 tbsp fish sauce

1-2 chillies, deseeded
and thinly sliced

2 tomatoes, cored and diced

To garnish
4 hard-boiled free-range eggs

½ telegraph cucumber, diced

150g mung bean sprouts

coriander and/or mint leaves

To make Laksa Base, heat oil in a large pot and sizzle the ginger, garlic, laksa paste and lime zest for a few seconds. Add the stock, coconut cream, sugar, fish sauce, chillies and tomatoes. Simmer 10 minutes. Laksa Base can be prepared ahead to this point and chilled or frozen until required.

When ready to serve, cook udon noodles in a separate pot according to packet instructions.

While the noodles are cooking, bring Laksa Base to a simmer, add fish, cover and simmer gently until fish is cooked through (about 5 minutes). Taste and adjust seasonings if required.

Drain noodles and divide between 4 bowls. Spoon fish and broth over the noodles. Cut peeled hard-boiled eggs in half lengthwise and add two halves to each bowl. Place cucumber, bean sprouts and coriander and/or mint on a platter so everyone can help themselves. The combination of crunchy greens and hot soup is fantastic.

Roast Chicken Platter with Rocket and Lemon

What could be easier and more delicious for a casual lunch or dinner than a platter of juicy roast chicken pieces topped with rocket leaves and lemon, then served with a spoonful of nutty pesto and a loaf of crusty bread. If you're strapped for time, start with a store-bought rotisserie chicken.

Prep time	15 mins
Cook time	60-75 mins
	+ resting
Serves	4-6

1 large free-range chicken (about 1.5kg)

olive oil, to brush or spray

2 tbsp melted butter

4 juicy lemons

salt and ground black pepper

2 handfuls (50g) rocket leaves

Heat oven to 220°C. Dry chicken inside and out with paper towels and remove visible fat. Place breast-side up in a deep oven dish that has been brushed or sprayed with a little olive oil.

Brush melted butter over chicken. Cut 1 lemon in half, squeeze the juice over the chicken and place the 2 squeezed lemon halves in the chicken cavity. Season chicken with salt and pepper. Roast 20-30 minutes or until chicken starts to brown.

Brush with pan liquids then cook a further 40-45 minutes until juices run clear when a skewer is inserted into the densest part of the thigh, or until a kitchen thermometer reaches 82°C when placed deep into the thigh. Allow chicken to rest for 10-15 minutes or up to 30 minutes.

When ready to serve, transfer chicken to a board and cut into large pieces. Arrange on a platter and sprinkle with rocket leaves. Cut the remaining three lemons into segments or cheeks and arrange around the platter.

Warm Chicken Liver Salad with Hazelnuts

To toast and skin the hazelnuts for this recipe, place them on a baking tray and bake at 180°C for 10 minutes. Cool, then place in a clean teatowel and rub to loosen the skins. Toasted nuts will keep in a sealed jar for several weeks – they're great to add to muesli or use in muffins or cakes.

Prep time	10 mins
Cook time	10 mins
Serves	4 as a starter or 2 as a main

300-350g free-range chicken livers

salt and ground black pepper

2 tbsp neutral oil

4 rashers streaky bacon, cut into 2cm pieces

2 tsp butter

3 handfuls (75g) baby spinach or rocket or watercress sprigs

2 oranges, peeled and segmented

2 tbsp hazelnuts, toasted, roughly skinned and coarsely chopped

1 tbsp lemon juice

a drizzle of pomegranate molasses (optional)

Devein and trim the chicken livers, cutting any large pieces in half. Season with salt and pepper.

Heat oil in a large, heavy-based frypan and fry bacon pieces until they start to crisp. Lift out of pan and set aside to cool.

Add butter to same pan and when it turns nut brown add the seasoned chicken livers. Cook over high heat, turning once, until browned but still lightly pink in the centre (about 2 minutes on one side and 1 minute on the other). Lift out of pan and set aside with the bacon.

Arrange spinach, rocket or watercress on a serving platter with oranges and chopped hazelnuts. Add warm bacon and chicken livers and gently toss. Drizzle with lemon juice and pomegranate molasses, if using, season to taste with salt and pepper and serve immediately.

Prawn and Bean Salad

I like to make this with whole prawns, which I boil briefly until they turn pink. Then I remove the shells and heads, leaving a little tip of the tail. It is a bit of a fiddle but they taste sweeter. If you're short of time, just choose the biggest prawn tails you can find. I prefer to use fat, juicy Australian prawns when possible.

Prep time	15 mins
Cook time	3-5 mins
Serves	4

24 large cooked whole prawns or prawn tails

4 tbsp olive oil

2 cloves garlic, crushed

finely grated zest of 1 lemon

1 tsp smoked paprika

2 x 400g cans butter beans, rinsed and drained

3 tbsp lemon juice

2 spring onions, finely chopped

5 medium tomatoes, cored and cut into small wedges

½ cup chopped coriander leaves

Remove shells from whole prawns, if using, leaving the tips of the tails intact. (If the heads are meaty, squeeze any juices into a bowl with the prawns to add extra flavour. You can also use the shells and heads to make stock.)

Heat oil in a medium-sized pot with garlic, lemon zest and paprika. Sizzle for 1-2 minutes without browning garlic.

Add prawns and drained beans and heat for 2-3 minutes, shaking the pot now and then. Remove from the heat and stir in lemon juice. Add spring onions, tomatoes and coriander and mix gently to combine. Transfer to a serving dish and serve at room temperature.

To market, to market

No matter where in the world I find myself, if there's a farmers' market nearby I'll be there. There is no better way to immerse yourself in the local food culture and connect with the environment at hand than at a farmers' market.

Even if my city garden is in full swing, I still like to head out on a Saturday morning to the two farmers' markets near our house. One is small with just a handful of local growers selling their fresh harvests, while the other is a hubbub of shoppers and traders from near and far. Turkish bread and olives line up next to freshly smoked salmon, home-made dips and spreads, French-style patés, Indian samosas, preserves, breads, cheeses and fresh fruit and vegetables. You can travel the world in the tastes on offer and seeing all that fresh produce makes me want to rush home and spend the afternoon cooking.

Farmers' markets make cities better places. There's always a buzz and bustle that brings you into the orbit of the local food culture and syncs you into the season's freshest fruit and vegetable harvests.

At farmers' markets there is an openness about sharing ideas and knowledge that you don't often find elsewhere. The lady behind you at the stall with the fat, sweet fennel bulbs has a brilliant idea for a fennel salad that you just have to go home and try (finely slice, salt and rinse the fennel, then dress with a vinaigrette of champagne vinegar, mustard and olive oil and toss with olives and sliced oranges).

The fennel grower shares his own ideas (slow-bake the fennel under a shoulder of pork with apples, white wine, thyme and rosemary). In these cross-cultural culinary exchanges your repertoire of cooking ideas and recipes expands, and with it your openness to other cultures, ingredients and tastes.

Many farmers' markets limit eligibility to growers who produce their food within a certain region, county or distance from the market. That's certainly what I expect when I visit a farmers' market, for in this ethos there is a true sense of a local food community and a provenance you can trust.

Perennial herbs $5.00

Warming Winter Soups

There are few more pleasurable ways to spend a winter morning than stirring a steaming pot of soup and having the kitchen fill up with its feel-good smell. It's such a nurturing meal to cook and enjoy together.

Tomato, Bacon and Bean Soup

Heat 2 tbsp olive oil in a large pot, add 6 finely diced rashers bacon (or leave this out for a vegetarian version), 1 diced green or red pepper, 2 diced medium onions, ½ tsp smoked paprika and 3 cloves crushed garlic and cook over medium heat until onions are softened but not browned. Add 1 tbsp tomato paste and 1 tsp sugar and cook another minute. Rinse and drain 2 x 400g cans butter beans, then add to pot with 500ml vegetable stock, 1 tsp chopped thyme, 1 tsp chopped rosemary and 2 x 400g cans tomatoes in juice. Cover and simmer 45 minutes. Season, garnish with chopped coriander or parsley and serve with grated parmesan. Serves 6 as a starter or 4 as a meal.

Roasted Cauliflower and Blue Cheese Soup

Cut 1 cauliflower into florets and place in a roasting dish with 2 tbsp butter, 1 cup vegetable or chicken stock and salt and white pepper to taste. Roast at 180°C, turning after 20 minutes. Cook until tender and just starting to caramelise around the edges (another 20-30 minutes). While cauliflower is cooking, dice 4 rashers bacon (optional) and fry until crispy. Toast and roughly chop ½ cup hazelnuts (see page 78). Purée cooked cauliflower with its cooking juices until smooth, then transfer to a large pot. Add 5 cups vegetable or chicken stock, 100g crumbled blue cheese, 3 tbsp chopped parsley, 2 cups milk and ½ cup cream. Bring to a simmer, stirring, and adjust seasonings to taste. Spoon into serving bowls and garnish with bacon, if using, and hazelnuts. Serves 6.

Lentil, Kumara and Watercress Soup

Boil 1 cup le puy or beluga lentils in unsalted water for 10 minutes. Drain and set aside. Heat 3 tbsp olive oil in a large pot and add 2 diced medium onions, 2 crushed cloves garlic, the finely grated zest of 1 lemon and 2 tbsp grated fresh ginger. Cook over a medium heat until onion is softened but not browned. Add lentils, 3 medium peeled and diced kumara (750g), 2 litres vegetable stock, 2 tbsp soy sauce and 1 tbsp honey. Cover and simmer until kumara is tender (about 25 minutes). Purée half the soup and return to pot. Just before serving, add 4 handfuls (100g) watercress leaves and 3 tbsp lemon juice. Season to taste and serve at once. Serves 6.

Smoky Io Soup

Simmering a ham hock long and slow for a couple of hours, then using the cooking liquid as a stock for the soup, is something our grandmothers used to do and it's a great way of making a little of a cheap cut go a long way. Chipotle chillies add a lovely smokiness, but the soup is still excellent without them.

Prep time	15 mins
	+ soaking
Cook time	2 hours
	40 mins
Serves	4-6

1 ham hock

2 dried chipotle chillies (optional)

2 tbsp olive oil

2 onions, finely diced

2 cloves garlic, crushed

1 tsp fennel seeds, roughly crushed

1 tsp cumin seeds, roughly crushed

1 tsp smoked paprika

2 chorizo sausages, thinly sliced

2 x 400g cans of beans, such as cannellini and red kidney beans, rinsed and drained

400g can chopped tomatoes in juice

salt and ground black pepper

Place ham hock in a large soup pot, cover with water and bring to a boil. Cover and simmer for about 2 hours, adding more water if needed.

While ham is cooking, pour ½ cup boiling water over dried chipotle chillies, if using, and leave to soak for 30 minutes.

Lift ham hock out of liquid, reserving liquid. Cool ham and cut into small chunks, discarding skin and fat.

Heat oil in a large pot and gently cook onions with garlic, fennel seeds, cumin seeds and smoked paprika until softened but not browned (about 5 minutes). Add chorizo and chopped ham and cook another 1-2 minutes. If using chipotle chillies, lift out of soaking liquid and chop, discarding seeds. Add to soup with their soaking liquid.

Add beans and tomatoes to the pot along with 3 cups of the cooking liquid from the ham hocks. Cover and simmer for 30 minutes to develop flavours.

When ready to serve, adjust seasoning to taste and divide among serving bowls.

Chicken and Prawn Gumbo

My take on this traditional Cajun and Creole meal combines chicken with okra, chorizo and prawns in a rich, dark sauce. Don't hurry the step when you brown the flour in the oil – this cooked roux base gives the gumbo its satisfying flavour.

Prep time	25 mins
Cook time	45-60 mins
Serves	6

8-10 skinless chicken thighs, bone in

salt and ground black pepper

1 tsp chopped rosemary

¼ cup neutral oil

3 tbsp flour

1 large onion, chopped

2 stalks celery, thinly sliced

1 red pepper, deseeded and diced

1 green pepper, deseeded and diced

4 cloves garlic, crushed

2 chorizo sausages, diced

1½ tbsp cajun spice mix

1 tbsp worcestershire sauce

350g okra, sliced

1 litre chicken stock

2 bay leaves

300g raw prawn tails

To serve
cooked rice

If cooking in oven, preheat to 160°C.

Season chicken pieces with salt, pepper and rosemary. Heat 2 tbsp of the oil over medium-high heat in a heavy-based soup pot or cast-iron casserole dish. Brown chicken well, working in batches if necessary so as not to overcrowd the pan, then lift out and set aside.

Add remaining 2 tbsp oil to pan, sprinkle in the flour and cook over medium heat for about 5 minutes, whisking constantly until it turns medium brown – almost the colour of milk chocolate. Add onion, celery, red and green pepper, garlic, chorizo and cajun spice mix to pan and cook over medium-low heat, stirring with a wooden spoon, until softened (about 3 minutes).

Stir in worcestershire sauce, okra, stock and bay leaves, then bury the chicken pieces in the sauce. Cover and bake in oven for 1 hour or simmer on stovetop for 45 minutes. Chicken and Prawn Gumbo can be prepared in advance to this stage, stored in the fridge for up to 48 hours and reheated when required.

When ready to serve, bring back to a simmer, mix in prawn tails and continue to cook until prawns turn pink (about 5 minutes). Adjust seasonings to taste. To serve, place rice in a large, deep serving dish and spoon gumbo on top.

It might be just another day, but
it's a day you'll never have again.
Make every moment matter.

Pack a picnic

I never need an excuse to eat outdoors. It's a great way to bring some of the pleasures of country life into an urban lifestyle.

Even on a cold, blustery day I can be found rugged up with my picnic in hand, heading off for a brisk walk up the hill at the end of our city street to meet a friend over a thermos of tea or a glass of wine and a simple sandwich or snack. It's such an invigorating way of blowing out all those computer-screen cobwebs.

You can jazz up your picnic with all manner of deli treats or, if you have the time, bake something portable to take along. But if I'm on the run I'll often just grab a loaf of french bread and some cheese and fruit. It's less about messing around with fancy food and more about getting outdoors, away from technology and pavements, and connecting with nature.

Thinking back to when our children were little and remembering that state of constant exhaustion that seems to overwhelm the lives of every new parent, I have no doubt that what got us through

without going barmy was getting outside as often as we could to picnic and barbecue. After a frenzied day of juggling work and young kids, Ted and I would pack a little hamper with bread and tomato sauce and sausages and head off with our picnic rug and portable barbecue to the nearest park. Sometimes I'd go to the effort of making a pie or a salad, but the sausages were always what the kids liked best.

I'd throw in a gesture to nutrition with a few pieces of fruit and salad veg (the kids never ate the veg), and I'd make sure I packed a bottle of wine and some cheese and olives for us harried parents.

The kids would wear themselves out roly-polying down the hill and happily gobble up their hot sausages wrapped in bread, thinking it was all a great adventure.

In the meantime, Ted and I would relax over a glass of wine, have a chat and shake off the day. Everyone would go home feeling wonderfully freed-up and relaxed. The kids slept like angels after these little urban picnic adventures.

Potato and Feta Picnic Pie

This hearty pie makes great fare for a picnic or casual lunch. Tailor your own version by adding your favourite flavours – try fresh tarragon or pesto in place of spring onion, chopped olives in place of capers, or parmesan or blue cheese instead of feta. Or glam it up with a layer of thinly sliced smoked salmon.

Prep time	25 mins
Cook time	90 mins
Serves	8

2 sheets flaky puff pastry

1kg potatoes,
peeled and thinly sliced

2 spring onions, thinly sliced

250g creamy feta

4 eggs

250ml milk

2 cloves garlic, crushed

1 tsp thyme leaves

2 tbsp chopped capers

2 tsp wholegrain mustard

1 tsp salt

ground black pepper

Preheat oven to 190°C. Place a baking tray in the oven and lightly grease a 25cm pie dish.

Roll out pastry sheets very thinly on a lightly floured board. Cover the base and sides of the pie dish with one sheet of pastry, overlapping the sides. Layer potato slices into the pastry shell, sprinkling a few spring onion slices and crumbling a little feta over each layer.

Beat eggs and milk together, reserving 1 tbsp to brush over the finished pie. Add garlic, thyme, capers, mustard, salt and pepper and mix to combine. Pour evenly over potatoes. Cover with the other sheet of pastry and press down around the edges firmly to seal. Trim off any excess pastry and use to garnish the pie.

Brush top of pie with reserved egg mixture. Place onto heated baking tray (this helps to crisp up the base) and bake for 45 minutes. Lower heat to 160°C and bake until the potatoes are tender (about a further 45 minutes). To check whether the potatoes are cooked, insert a skewer into the centre of the pie – if they are done the skewer will not meet any resistance.

Serve the pie hot or warm. Any leftovers can be refrigerated and reheated the next day.

Smoked Salmon and Egg Gratin

My friend Emerald introduced me to this easy dish, which is based on a recipe from her friend Fran. I love the way these things go around – when something tastes good everyone wants to share it! You could add a mashed potato or crumb topping, or even layer some wilted spinach through the eggs and salmon.

Prep time	20 mins
Cook time	15-20 mins
Serves	4 as a main or
	5-6 as lunch

600g boneless, skinless hot-smoked salmon or other smoked fish

6 hard-boiled free-range eggs, peeled and halved

2 tsp worcestershire sauce

1 tbsp tomato sauce

a pinch of cayenne

a sprinkle of paprika

White Sauce
70g butter

½ cup flour

a pinch of nutmeg

3½ cups milk

salt and fine white pepper

To serve
crisp green salad

To make White Sauce, melt butter in a medium pot. When butter starts to bubble, add flour and stir over heat for about 1 minute. Add nutmeg, then gradually whisk in milk, stirring until a thick, smooth sauce is produced. Season to taste (it should be well seasoned). White Sauce will keep in the fridge for 3-4 days. It will thicken as it cools, so cover the top with baking paper so it doesn't dry out or form a skin.

To make the gratin, flake salmon or other smoked fish into large chunks and arrange in the base of a medium baking dish. Arrange the hard-boiled egg halves on top.

Stir worcestershire sauce, tomato sauce and cayenne into the White Sauce and spread evenly over the top of the fish and eggs. Sprinkle with paprika. If not serving at once, cover and chill – it will keep for at least 24 hours in the fridge. Bring to room temperature before baking.

When you are ready to serve, bake at 220°C until the sauce is bubbling and the top is lightly golden (about 15-20 minutes). Serve hot with a crisp green salad on the side.

Sensational Spinach Tart

My mother made this savoury tart often, and it's still the best I've tasted. It has a denser texture than a quiche and wonderful green colour. I've doubled the recipe so you can freeze one for later – they freeze beautifully. If you don't have five minutes to whizz up pastry in the food processor, use frozen savoury pastry sheets.

Prep time	20 mins
Cook time	45 mins
Makes	2 medium tarts

1 cup (250g) cream cheese

6 eggs

1 cup cream or milk

2 tbsp pesto

2 spring onions, chopped

2 tsp horseradish sauce

1 cup grated cheese

4-6 heads fresh spinach (use as much or as little as you like)

salt and ground black pepper

¼ tsp freshly grated nutmeg

Food-Processor Pastry
2 cups flour

½ tsp salt

150g butter
or 75g butter and 75g lard

about 4 tbsp cold water

Preheat oven to 200°C and line two 26-28cm loose-bottomed quiche dishes with baking paper.

To make the Food-Processor Pastry, place the flour, salt and butter or butter and lard in a food processor and whizz to fine crumbs. With the motor running, add the water a little at a time, adding more if necessary until mixture comes together in a ball.

Press pastry into the base and sides of the quiche dishes, cover with baking paper, weight with baking beans or rice and bake blind until lightly golden (about 12-15 minutes).

While pastry cooks, prepare the filling. Blend together the cream cheese, eggs and cream or milk. Add pesto, spring onions, horseradish, cheese, spinach, salt, pepper and nutmeg, blending until the mixture forms a smooth, green purée.

Remove pastry shells from oven and lift off baking paper and baking beans, cooling and reserving for later reuse. Reduce oven heat to 180°C. Pour filling mixture into the semi-cooked pastry shells and bake for about 30 minutes until it is set in the centre and lightly golden. Serve warm or hot.

To reheat from frozen, remove from freezer at least 1 hour before serving and place on an oven tray lined with baking paper. Bake at 160°C until warmed through (about 15-20 minutes).

A Smoked Chicken in the Fridge...

Smoked chicken is the starting point for all manner of meals – from pies to pastas. It's also great in salads, soups and sandwiches.

Hearty Smoked Chicken Chowder

Heat 3 tbsp butter in a large pot and gently cook 2 finely diced onions, 2 finely diced stalks celery and 2 diced carrots until softened but not browned (about 8 minutes). Add 6 cups water, 2 diced potatoes, shredded flesh of ½ smoked chicken, 2 bay leaves, a sprig of thyme, salt and white pepper. Cover and simmer about 30 minutes. Add 1½ cups canned, frozen or fresh corn kernels. Mix 3 tbsp cornflour with a little milk, then stir in the rest of 1 cup milk. Add to soup and cook 3-4 minutes, stirring, until slightly thickened (roughly mash for a thicker texture). Mix in 3 tbsp chopped parsley and adjust seasonings to taste. Serves 6.

Quick Smoked Chicken Pasta

Cook 400g dried pasta according to packet instructions. Drain, reserving 1 cup cooking water. While pasta cooks, heat 3 tbsp olive oil in a frypan, add 3-4 chopped rashers bacon and cook 2 minutes. Add 400g sliced button mushrooms and cook a further 2 minutes. Add to drained pasta with 1 thinly sliced smoked chicken breast, 250g crème fraiche, reserved cooking water, finely grated zest of 1 lemon and 2 tbsp chopped parsley and allow to heat through. Serves 4.

Smoked Chicken and Mustard Pie

Preheat oven to 200°C and place a baking tray in the oven to heat. Place 1 sheet of flaky pastry on a piece of baking paper, dust with a little flour and roll out until you can cut it into a circle 24cm in diameter (use a cake tin or plate as a guide). In a bowl, combine 400g shredded smoked chicken, 250g sour cream, finely grated zest of ½ a lemon, 1 tsp lemon juice, 2 tbsp wholegrain mustard, 2 tbsp chopped parsley and salt and pepper to taste. Spread over pastry, leaving a 2cm border. Brush border with a little lightly beaten egg. Roll out a second sheet of flaky pastry a little larger than the first, until you can cut it into a circle 25cm in diameter (to allow for the height of the filling). Place over filling and press down edges with a fork to seal. Brush top with beaten egg and pierce in 2-3 places with a sharp knife. Slide baking paper and pie onto hot oven tray and bake for 20-25 minutes until golden. Serve warm or at room temperature. Serves 4-6.

Carrot Cake for a Crowd

This moist, flavoursome cake is incredibly simple to make and always earns compliments. Add ½ cup raisins and ¼ cup chopped walnuts if you wish.

Prep time   10 mins
Cook time   55-60 mins
Makes   1 large cake

1 cup neutral oil

2 cups raw or white sugar

4 eggs

1 cup wholemeal flour

1 cup plain flour

¼ tsp salt

2 tsp cinnamon

1 tsp mixed spice

1 tsp ground ginger

3 cups grated carrot
(about 3 medium carrots)

2 tsp baking soda

1 tbsp orange juice

Cream Cheese Icing
75g butter, softened
but not melted

250g cream cheese
(not low-fat)

finely grated zest and juice
of 1 lemon, or more to taste

4 cups icing sugar

To garnish
fine strands of orange zest

Preheat oven to 160°C. Grease a 25cm springform cake tin and line with baking paper.

Place oil, sugar and eggs in a food processor, electric mixer or mixing bowl and whizz or beat to combine. Add wholemeal flour, plain flour, salt, cinnamon, mixed spice, ginger and grated carrot. Pulse or mix until just combined – don't overmix. Dissolve baking soda in orange juice and pulse or stir into cake mixture.

Spread into prepared tin and bake until the cake is springy to the touch and a skewer inserted into the midde comes out clean (about 55-60 minutes). Allow to cool in tin for 10-15 minutes before turning out onto a cake rack. The uniced cake will keep in an airtight container in a cool place for up to a week. When you are ready to serve, ice with Cream Cheese Icing.

To make Cream Cheese Icing, place butter, cream cheese, lemon zest and juice and icing sugar in a food processor or bowl. Whizz or beat until smooth then spread over top and sides of cake. Garnish with orange zest.

Lemon Coconut Cake

This recipe is based on a lemon cake recipe I've been making for years. One day I threw in a handful of coconut and found it tasted better than ever. It's a huge, wonderfully moist cake that you can whizz together in a food processor in a flash.

Prep time	5 mins
Cook time	1½ hours
Makes	1 large cake

3 cups sugar

4 eggs

finely grated zest
and juice of 4 lemons

2 cups neutral oil

1¾ cups plain
unsweetened yoghurt

½ cup desiccated coconut

4 cups self-raising flour

a pinch of salt

Coconut Icing
75g butter, softened
but not melted

250g cream cheese
(not low-fat)

½ tsp coconut essence

½ cup desiccated coconut

4 cups icing sugar

Preheat oven to 160°C. Grease a 28-30cm springform cake tin and line with baking paper.

Place sugar, eggs, lemon zest and juice, oil and yoghurt in a food processor, electric mixer or mixing bowl and whizz or beat until combined. Add coconut, flour and salt and pulse or mix until only just combined – do not overmix.

Transfer to prepared cake tin and bake until the cake is springy to the touch and a skewer inserted into the midde comes out clean (about 1½ hours). Cool in tin before turning out and icing.

To make Coconut Icing, place butter, cream cheese, coconut essence, desiccated coconut and icing sugar in a food processor or bowl and whizz or beat until smooth. If icing is too runny to spread, chill until it reaches a spreadable consistency then spread over top and sides of cake.

Sweet Little Tartlets

It's handy to have cooked sweet pastry cases in the pantry. You can buy ready-made cases or make your own from frozen shortcrust pastry sheets. If you want to make Sweet Shortcrust Pastry from scratch, see my recipe on page 300.
If I'm caught short, I just use good-quality shortbread biscuits to make mini tarts!

Fresh Fruit Tartlets with Mascarpone Cream

To make Mascarpone Cream, stir together 250g mascarpone, 1 tsp vanilla extract, 3 tbsp icing sugar, the finely grated zest of 1 lemon and ½ tsp ground cloves. Fill 24 cooked sweet pastry tartlet cases with Mascarpone Cream. Top with seasonal fresh fruit such as berries or sliced stone fruit. Arrange on a platter or cake stand and serve within 2 hours of filling. Makes 24.

Strawberry Custard Tarts

To make Fast Custard Filling, measure ½ cup mascarpone and 1 cup store-bought vanilla custard. Mix 2 tbsp of the custard into the mascarpone to soften it a little, then stir in remaining custard and the finely grated zest of ½ a lemon. Spoon into eight 9-10cm diameter cooked sweet pastry cases. Top with strawberry slices and brush with a little sieved raspberry jam to glaze. Makes 8.

Raspberry Jam Shortbreads

Spread raspberry jam onto 12 shortbread biscuits and place on a pretty serving dish or cake stand. Top each with a fresh raspberry and serve. Makes 12.

Roasted Plum Tarts

Halve 9 fresh plums and remove stones. Place cut-side up in a shallow baking dish, drizzle with 2 tbsp honey and ¼ cup water and bake at 250°C until plums are slightly browned and juices have caramelised (about 10 minutes). If using canned plums, drain 1 cup of the juices into a pot, add 2 tbsp honey and simmer until reduced to a thick syrup. Cool. To make Creamy Yoghurt Filling, combine 6 tbsp greek yoghurt with 3 tbsp sour cream and 1 tbsp honey. Just before serving, spoon filling into 9-10cm diameter baked sweet pastry shells, top each with 3 plum halves and drizzle with caramelised plum syrup. Makes 6.

A Long Lunch on a Cold Day

Ward off winter's chills with big flavours and the comfort of home-cooked soup. Most of this meal can be made in advance – it's a piece of cake.

Broccoli, Blue Cheese and Almond Tarts, page 251

Smoky Jo Soup, page 89

Crusty bread

Salad of Beets, Beans and Walnuts, page 52

Lemon Coconut Cake, page 106

Coffee

Chilled chenin blanc

Lunch with the Girls

A summer lunch with the girls calls for light, zingy dishes with some indulgent ingredients – and a glass or two of bubbly, of course.

🍴🥄

Scallops with Lemon Caper Butter, page 164

෴

Duck and Mango Salad, page 72

෴

Strawberry Custard Tarts, page 108

෴

Chilled bubbly

For prep plans, shopping lists and more menus
see annabel-langbein.com

dinner in minutes

The best fast food doesn't come from a takeaway bar.

When YouTube started up, I remember going online one weeknight to see if there were any clever ideas for the pile of eggplants I had on hand. I came upon a video for an eggless eggplant frittata, which seemed an interesting, authentic recipe and looked easy and appetising. All those boxes – tick, tick, tick – I was onto it.

Two and a half hours later the kitchen looked like a war zone and the family was mutinying. When we finally did sit down to eat, the so-called frittata was truly awful – nothing like the lovely golden thing on the screen. It stuck to the pan and was gloopy and tasteless. Talk about demoralising. But my lesson was learnt – when you want a meal in a hurry, stick with easy methods and simple ingredients.

If you start with a really fresh piece of chicken or fish or some well-aged meat and apply an ethnic sauce, spice rub or paste from your global pantry, you can then use the cooking method of your choice (pan-fry or stir-fry, oven-bake or roast) and make a pan sauce or toss in some deli fixings from the pantry or fridge. It's a fast and foolproof strategy for getting great food on the table without really having to think, and means that day in, day out, you can create interesting meals just by rotating the cooking methods, protein and vegetables, and changing the flavourings. This is my formula for speed dining at home – it takes less time than a trip to the takeaway bar and is better for your health and your pocket.

Midweek we usually opt for fresh fruit rather than dessert but it's fun to make a personalised ice cream using store-bought ice cream as a base. Play around with the flavours – I love the old-fashioned sweets of my childhood, such as Jaffas and Crunchie bars, crushed and folded through, but I have no doubt that you'll come up with your own fabulous favourite combinations.

Easy First-Course Assembles

Adding a quickly assembled first course is an easy way of transforming an ordinary midweek meal into something a bit special, or making a family meal go further if you have unexpected visitors just on dinnertime.

Tomatoes Stuffed with Chèvre and Mint

Cut the lids off 4 medium tomatoes and scoop the flesh and seeds into a strainer over a small bowl, leaving the shells intact. Mix 100g goat cheese with 1 tbsp chopped mint and 2 tbsp juice from the strained tomatoes (discard seeds and pulp). Remove seeds from ½ lebanese cucumber and finely chop the flesh. Mix half of this into the cheese mixture, pile into the tomato shells and garnish with remaining diced cucumber. Serves 4 as a starter or 2 as a light lunch with crusty bread.

Cucumber Salad with Salmon and Lemon Chive Yoghurt

Prepare pickled cucumber by very finely slicing 1 lebanese cucumber and 1 small bulb fennel (or use 2 lebanese cucumbers). Mix 1 tsp sugar, ½ tsp salt, ¼ tsp fine white pepper, 1 tbsp white wine vinegar and 3 tbsp boiling water. Pour over cucumber and fennel and stand for 15 minutes or up to 24 hours in the fridge. Drain before serving. To make Lemon Chive Yoghurt, mix 4 tbsp greek yoghurt, 1 tsp chopped chives, 1 tsp horseradish sauce, 2 tsp lemon juice and salt and pepper to taste. Arrange 3-4 slices cold-smoked salmon on plates with a mound of cucumber salad and a dollop of Lemon Chive Yoghurt. Garnish with fennel or chives. Serves 4 as a starter.

Baked Ricotta and Pine Nuts

Mix together 500g ricotta, the finely grated zest of 1 large lemon, 2 tbsp lemon juice, 2 fat cloves garlic crushed with 1 tsp salt, ½ cup coarsely grated parmesan and a little ground black pepper. Mix in 2 lightly whisked eggs and 1 tsp fresh thyme leaves. Spoon the mixture into a 3 cup capacity oiled baking dish, sprinkle with 3 tbsp pine nuts and bake at 180°C for 30 minutes. Allow to cool, then chill for at least an hour before serving with crusty bread. Serves 4 as a starter. Baked Ricotta keeps for about a week in the fridge and is also good served with salad.

Beef Pho

This is my go-to meal after a busy day when I'm too tired to cook. You can make it with chicken stock and chicken if you prefer but you'll need to simmer the chicken in the broth to fully cook it through before adding it to the noodles.

Prep time	15 mins
Cook time	8 mins
Serves	4 as a starter
	or 2 as a main

100g dried rice vermicelli

1 litre good-quality beef stock

2 cups water

1½ tbsp fish sauce

½ tsp five-spice powder

a pinch of ground cloves

1 tbsp grated fresh ginger

½-1 long red chilli, deseeded

1 kaffir lime leaf
or finely grated zest of 1 lime

4 button mushrooms, sliced

1 stalk lemongrass (optional)

100-150g beef fillet, trimmed

2 spring onions

1 medium carrot

2 tbsp chopped coriander

2-4 tbsp lime or lemon juice

To serve
coriander leaves

lime cheeks

sliced fresh chillies (optional)

Place rice vermicelli noodles in a bowl, cover with boiling water and leave to soak for 10 minutes. While they soak, place stock in a pot with water, fish sauce, five-spice powder, cloves, ginger, finely chopped chilli, lime leaf or zest and mushrooms. Bruise the lemongrass stalk, if using, with a rolling pin and add to the pot. Bring to a boil and simmer for 5 minutes.

While the broth is cooking, cut the beef fillet across the grain into the thinnest possible slices. To prepare the garnish, cut spring onions and carrot into 5cm lengths and then shred finely.

Drain noodles, snip with scissors in a few places for easy eating and divide between heated bowls. Top with raw beef slices and coriander. Remove lemongrass stalk and lime leaf, if using, from broth, adjust seasonings to taste and divide boiling broth between bowls (it will lightly cook the beef). Drizzle each bowl with 1 tbsp lime or lemon juice and top with shredded spring onion and carrot.

Garnish with coriander leaves and lime wedges and serve at once. If desired, accompany with a bowl of sliced chillies.

Tunisian Chicken Salad with Orange Dressing

If you're pressed for time, buy a rotisserie chicken for a speedy assembly of this luscious salad. Alternatively, gently poach 4 single chicken breasts using my Perfect Poached Chicken method on page 140. When apricots aren't in season I'll use grapes, pear slices or orange segments.

Prep time   15 mins
Serves   4-6

1 roasted free-range chicken

2 medium cos lettuces, torn into chunks

6 fresh apricots, destoned and cut into small wedges

2 spring onions, finely sliced

½ cup chopped pistachios

¼ cup finely chopped coriander or mint leaves

Orange Dressing
2 tsp ground cumin

1 tsp grated fresh ginger

2 tsp honey

4 tbsp fresh orange juice

finely grated zest and juice of 2 juicy lemons

4 tbsp olive oil

salt and ground black pepper

To make the Orange Dressing, shake together in a small jar the cumin, ginger, honey, orange juice, lemon zest and juice, oil and salt and pepper to taste.

To prepare the salad, strip the chicken from the bones, discarding skin and fat and reserving bones to make stock if desired. Roughly shred the flesh into bite-sized pieces. Place in a bowl and toss with half the Orange Dressing.

Place the cos lettuce in a serving bowl with apricot wedges, spring onions, pistachios and coriander or mint leaves.

When ready to serve, add the chicken and its dressing to the salad and toss gently with the remaining dressing.

Miso-Glazed Salmon

One or two oily fish meals each week will meet your needs for long-chain omega-3 fatty acids. Salmon makes a brilliant midweek meal because it cooks under the grill in a matter of minutes. Miso is a Japanese soybean paste that is rich in vitamin B. It's handy to have in your kitchen arsenal and it keeps in the fridge for months.

Prep time	5 mins
Cook time	10 mins
	+ standing
Serves	4

4 boneless, skinless salmon fillets (120-150g each)

2 tsp black and white sesame seeds

Miso Glaze
1½ tbsp miso, preferably white miso

1 tsp sesame oil

2 tbsp water

2 tsp soft brown sugar

Japanese-Style Rice
2 cups short-grain or sushi rice

4 tsp soy sauce

4 tsp butter

2 cloves garlic, crushed

3 cups water

To serve
4 heads bok choy, halved and lightly cooked

To cook Japanese-Style Rice, place rice in a pot with soy sauce, butter, garlic and water. Bring to a boil, stir and cover. Turn to lowest heat and cook for 10 minutes. Remove from heat without lifting the lid and leave to stand for 15-30 minutes.

To make the Miso Glaze, mix miso, sesame oil, water and sugar.

Preheat grill to high. Place salmon on a baking tray lined with tin foil (for easy washing up). Spread Miso Glaze over salmon and sprinkle with sesame seeds. Grill salmon 10cm from heat source without turning until lightly glazed and just cooked through (about 8 minutes). It should give when gently pressed.

To serve, fluff Japanese-Style Rice with a fork and spoon onto plates. Top each plate with a salmon fillet and 2 bok choy halves and serve immediately.

Fresh Fish in a Flash

Pick up some fresh white fish fillets on your way home and you have the starting point for all manner of meals. Fish takes only a few minutes to cook in a hot pan and the flavours you add can take your tastebuds anywhere in the world.

Cajun Fish Tacos

Mix 2 tbsp rice flour or plain flour and 3 tsp cajun spice mix in a shallow bowl. Dip 4-6 boneless, skinless white fish fillets in milk, shake off excess, then coat in seasoned flour. Heat 2 tbsp butter and 1 tbsp olive oil in a heavy-based frypan and fry fish over medium heat until cooked through (about 2 minutes each side). Serve with warm tortillas, shredded lettuce and an avocado mashed with a little lemon juice and salt and pepper. Garnish with lime cheeks and coriander sprigs. You could also include sliced cucumber and tomato if desired. Serves 4.

Pan-Fried Fish with Speedy Red Pepper Aioli

Season 2 tbsp flour with 1 tsp salt and pepper. Lightly coat 4-6 boneless, skinless fish fillets with seasoned flour, shaking off excess. Whisk 1 egg with 1 tbsp milk and dip floured fish into egg then into breadcrumbs or panko crumbs to coat. Refrigerate until required. To make Speedy Red Pepper Aioli, purée the flesh of 2 roasted red peppers with 2 cloves garlic, 2 tbsp lemon juice, ¾ cup good-quality mayonnaise and salt and pepper to taste. Heat 2 tbsp butter and 1 tbsp oil in a heavy-based frypan and fry fish over medium heat until golden and cooked through (about 2 minutes each side). Garnish with parsley and serve with Speedy Red Pepper Aioli, slaw and roast potatoes. Serves 4.

Sumac and Sesame Fish with Fennel Salad

To make Fennel Salad, squeeze the juice of 1 lemon into a small bowl of cold water. Cut 1 fennel bulb in half and slice each half lengthwise as thinly as possible. Place into the acidulated water to prevent browning. Very finely slice a small red onion and add to the water along with a small handful of italian parsley leaves and a small handful of curly endive or lettuce. Peel and segment 2 grapefruit. Lightly sprinkle both sides of 4-6 boneless, skinless white fish fillets with sumac, black sesame seeds and salt and pepper. Heat 2 tbsp butter and 1 tbsp neutral oil in a heavy-based frypan and fry fish over medium heat until cooked through (about 2 minutes each side). Drain Fennel Salad and toss with grapefruit. Divide between plates and top with fish to serve. Serves 4.

The urban pantry

Each day more than 200,000 people around the world make the move from countryside to city. Often they bring with them little more than their language, whatever fragments of culture can be mustered and the memories of another life. In this swirling diaspora, the world's pantry arrives on our doorstep, broadening our culinary horizons and invigorating our palates. Soon, once-exotic flavours assume familiarity and ingredients such as pomegranate molasses, tahini, sesame oil, balsamic vinegar and curry paste find their way into our shopping baskets. Having this global pantry at our fingertips means we can take simple, everyday ingredients and easily create dishes that taste exotic and novel.

The freezer is a good place to keep small portions of bacon, a variety of breads and emergency quick-to-thaw protein such as chicken, steak or salmon fillets (its high fat content means salmon freezes better than other fish) that can be cooked quickly and tarted up. A pan-fried steak served on a bed of rocket with a drizzle of pomegranate molasses and a scatter of pistachios and dried cranberries is much more interesting than regular old steak and onions. Quickly

thawed chicken breasts can be smothered in a spicy rub, flash-baked or pan-fried and served with wilted bok choy and rice. Or pile chunks of feta, olives and roasted peppers onto fresh rocket or baby spinach with a handful of cherry tomatoes and a drizzle of balsamic vinaigrette, and serve toasted pita bread from the freezer on the side.

My pantry is always stocked with cans of pulses such as beans and chickpeas as well as tuna, anchovies, tomatoes and olives, and I keep plenty of sauces and condiments at hand to jazz things up. Also in the larder are long-life vegetables such as onions, garlic, ginger, potatoes and other root vegetables.

In the fridge I keep seasonal vegetables such as carrots, beets and parsnips in winter and salad greens in summer, dairy essentials such as yoghurt and butter, plus a few little treats – a wedge of favourite cheese or a piece of hot-smoked salmon.

On my kitchen bench I keep baskets of lemons, limes and other seasonal fruits, while on my windowsill are little pots of herbs, so no matter how pressed I am for time, I know that a fresh, flavoursome meal is only minutes away.

For more pantry tips see annabel-langbein.com

Creamy Mushroom Risotto

This handy storecupboard meal is great served with grilled chicken or steak. It's surprisingly quick and the way I make it requires hardly any stirring. Opinions differ on whether risotto should be sloppy like soup or slightly drier so it holds its shape in the bowl. I like mine sloppy – make yours as you prefer.

Prep time	10 mins
	+ soaking
Cook time	30 mins
Serves	4-5

5-6 slices dried mushroom, such as porcini

¾ cup dry white wine

6 tbsp butter

500g mixed fresh mushrooms, thinly sliced

1 small onion, finely diced

2 cloves garlic, crushed

1 tsp finely chopped rosemary leaves

finely grated zest of 1 lemon

2 cups arborio rice or other risotto rice

6 cups hot vegetable stock, or more if needed

salt and ground black pepper

juice of ½ a lemon

½ cup finely grated parmesan

Place dried mushrooms in a small bowl with ¼ cup of the wine and set aside to soak for at least 15 minutes. Heat 3 tbsp of the butter in a medium-large, heavy-based pot and gently cook fresh mushrooms until lightly browned. Add soaked dried mushrooms and their liquid, and cook until all the liquid has evaporated. Lift out of pot, season to taste and set aside.

Melt the remaining 3 tbsp butter in the same pot without washing and gently cook onion, garlic, rosemary and lemon zest until onion is clear but not browned (about 5 minutes). Add rice and stir over heat for 1 minute to lightly toast and coat the grains with butter. Add remaining ½ cup wine and cook until evaporated.

Add all the hot stock. Stir well, season to taste and cover with a lid. Bring to a boil then lower the heat and cook for 16 minutes, stirring occasionally and adding more stock or hot water, if needed, if the rice starts to get dry and stops looking like a soupy porridge. To check whether the rice is cooked, use the back of a knife to crush one of the grains – if it is cooked there will no longer be a hard, white core at the centre. When it is just cooked through, stir in the mushrooms, lemon juice and parmesan, adjust seasonings and serve.

What is it about some foods that makes them so soothing? Every culture has its own take on comfort food – often based around simple peasant fare.

Lime and Sesame Beef Stir-Fry

This is a great one-pot dinner you can make with storecupboard noodles and whatever fresh ingredients you have to hand. I like it with beef and broccoli. Depending on how hungry you are and how many mouths you have to feed, you could add another bundle of noodles to bulk it out.

Prep time   5 mins
Cook time   10 mins
Serves   2

250-300g lean beef, such as sirloin or rump steak

finely grated zest of 1 lime

2 cloves garlic, finely sliced

1 tbsp soy sauce

1 tsp sesame oil

270g-300g dried udon or soba noodles

1 head broccoli, cut into small florets, stem peeled

1 tbsp neutral oil

1 tbsp oyster sauce

2 tbsp water

1 head bok choy, leaves separated

1 handful (30g) snow peas

1 spring onion, finely sliced

2 tbsp toasted sesame seeds

2 tbsp lime juice

Trim any sinew or fat from the beef and discard. Slice beef as thinly as possible across the grain. Mix beef with lime zest, garlic, soy sauce and sesame oil. Leave to stand on the bench while you cook the noodles according to the instructions on the packet. Add broccoli to the noodle pot in the last 2 minutes of cooking. Tip noodles and broccoli into a colander and cool under cold water, then drain well.

Heat neutral oil in a wok or large frypan and stir-fry beef over high heat for 1 minute. Add oyster sauce, water, bok choy and snow peas and stir-fry for another minute.

Add drained noodles and broccoli to the frypan with the spring onion and sesame seeds. Toss over high heat to fully heat through (about 1-2 minutes), then stir in lime juice and pile into bowls or plates. Serve at once.

Stir-and-Serve Pasta

Pasta is the ultimate 10-minute meal. These sauces use mostly storecupboard ingredients and can be thrown together quickly while the pasta is in the pot.

Pasta with Spinach and Walnuts

Cook 200g dried pappardelle or fettuccine according to packet instructions. While pasta cooks, heat 2 tbsp olive oil in a large frypan and gently cook 2 crushed fat cloves garlic and grated zest of 1 lemon for 1-2 minutes. Add 300g bunch spinach, trimmed and chopped, cover and cook until wilted. Drain pasta, reserving ½ cup cooking liquid, and toss both in spinach mixture with 80g crumbled goat cheese, 50g grated parmesan and ½ cup toasted walnuts. Season to taste, divide between 2 bowls and drizzle 1 tbsp boutique extra virgin olive oil over each bowl. Serves 2.

Pronto Pasta with Pine Nuts and Tomatoes

Cook 400g dried pasta shapes according to packet instructions. While pasta cooks, heat 4 tbsp olive oil and fry 2 thinly sliced zucchini and 2 cloves crushed garlic over medium heat until they start to soften (2-3 minutes). Drain pasta. Toss with zucchini, ½ cup toasted pine nuts, 250g halved red and yellow cherry tomatoes, ¼ cup basil or other herb pesto thinned with olive oil, 100g crumbled feta cheese, 2 tbsp lemon juice and salt and pepper to taste. Serves 4.

Pasta with Salmon, Capers and Rocket

Cook 400g dried pappardelle or fettuccine according to packet instructions. While pasta cooks, remove bones and skin from 300g hot-smoked salmon and flake flesh coarsely. Heat 2 tbsp olive oil in a frypan and fry 3 tbsp capers until crunchy. Transfer to a plate. Add 200g baby rocket or spinach leaves to pan, season with salt and pepper and cook until wilted. Drain pasta and toss with capers, salmon, finely grated zest of 1 lemon, 2 tbsp boutique extra virgin olive oil and 2-3 tbsp lemon juice to taste. Adjust seasonings, divide between plates and top with rocket or spinach. Serves 4.

Ginger Chilli Sweet and Sour Chicken

I prefer chicken thigh quarters for this treatment as the meat is more flavoursome and it stays wonderfully succulent when baked. This combination of Asian flavours including chilli and ginger offers a new take on sweet and sour.

Prep time	10 mins
Cook time	35-40 mins
Serves	4

4 chicken marylands (thigh quarters) or 1 whole free-range chicken, quartered

salt and ground black pepper

2 tbsp neutral oil

3 tbsp sugar

3 tbsp white vinegar

½ cup white wine

1 cup chicken stock

½ long red chilli, deseeded and finely chopped, or more to taste

1½ tbsp grated fresh ginger

2 fat cloves garlic, chopped

1 tbsp fish sauce

To garnish (optional)
neutral oil, for frying

small handful mint, basil or vietnamese mint leaves

To serve
cooked rice

lightly cooked greens

Preheat oven to 200°C. Season chicken with salt and pepper. Heat oil in a large cast-iron baking dish and brown chicken all over, working in batches if necessary so as not to overcrowd the pan. Remove chicken and set aside.

Drain oil from the pan, add sugar and vinegar and cook over high heat until mixture starts to caramelise. Add wine, stock, chilli, ginger, garlic and fish sauce. Bring to a boil then return chicken to dish and cover with juices.

Bake uncovered, basting several times with the cooking liquids, until chicken is golden and fully cooked (about 35-40 minutes).

While chicken is baking, prepare the fried herb garnish, if using. Heat 2cm oil in a small pot until it shimmers and fry mint, basil or vietnamese mint leaves until they just change colour (about 5-10 seconds). Lift out with a slotted spoon and drain on paper towels.

Serve chicken with rice and lightly cooked greens, with any remaining cooking liquids spooned over the top. Garnish with fried herbs, if using.

No strawberry
ever tastes
sweeter than
one picked while
it's still warm
from the sun.

The edible backyard

Most of us crave a simpler existence, one that connects us to the rhythms of nature and the seasons. I have found the easiest way to do this in the city is to grow a garden where I can harvest some of my own food. Even if my pickings make only a small contribution to our meals, I feel like I am building some ownership around what I eat.

I am lucky to have a big backyard garden at my Auckland home. When we moved in 23 years ago, we were faced with a blank canvas, with not a tree on the property aside from an old monkey apple up the back. Now we are surrounded by established trees enclosing a thriving and productive garden – it's like a secret hideaway in the middle of the city.

The Auckland climate allows us to grow things I could never imagine growing down south in Wanaka. Throughout the year we harvest cherimoyas, feijoas, tamarillos, guavas, avocados, macadamias, citrus, pears, apples, plums and even bananas.

My vegetable potager always takes more planning than I think it will. I often forget to work backwards from the time I want to be harvesting. There is nothing more frustrating than having all your beans or tomatoes or zucchini close to being ready just as you are about to depart for three weeks' holiday. Or going to the market to find snow peas are in and you haven't even planted yours. Each plant takes a different length of time to mature and this will also be affected by the season and the heat in the ground.

Tomatoes are one of the most worthwhile vegetables to grow and they do really well (often better) in pots. Start them indoors and when all danger of frost has passed, put the pots outside. I like to plant basil underneath – it's a good companion for tomatoes, both in the ground and on the plate.

Whatever you grow, and on whatever scale, it will need water. In my experience, it's easy to forget – and then one day you go out and find everything is dead. (If plants are just wilted, a good, long soak will usually bring them back again in a few hours, but the more frequently they are stressed the more bitter they become.) If you're as forgetful as me, investing in a watering system or self-watering pots is a good idea. It means you will harvest sweet, tender vegetables and not face the despondency of consigning your efforts to the compost heap.

For more gardening advice see annabel-langbein.com

Chicken Tonnato

The classic Italian dish vitello tonnato involves veal with a tuna sauce. My version combines poached chicken breasts with a creamy tuna mayonnaise. It's quick to prepare if you poach the chicken in advance. The Tonnato Sauce also makes a great sandwich filling or you can add a little extra mayo to make a tasty dip.

Prep time	10 mins
Cook time	12 mins
	+ cooling
Serves	6

Perfect Poached Chicken
6 single boneless,
skinless chicken breasts

2 bay leaves

2-3 sprigs fresh thyme

1 lemon, thinly sliced

1 tsp salt

Tonnato Sauce
185g can tuna, drained

5 tbsp good-quality
mayonnaise

1 tbsp chopped capers

2 tbsp lemon juice

ground black pepper

1-2 tbsp water, to thin

To serve
lettuce leaves

chopped olives

sprigs of fresh thyme

To make Perfect Poached Chicken, place chicken breasts in a single layer in a large pot. Add bay leaves, thyme, lemon slices and salt and add water to cover chicken by 4cm. Place over medium-high heat and bring to a simmer. Reduce heat, cover and simmer for 5 minutes, then remove from heat and cool without uncovering for about 2 hours. If not using at once, the chicken can be stored in the stock in the fridge for up to 4 days.

When ready to serve, remove cooled chicken from stock (strain stock and reserve for later use). Cut chicken into finger-thick slices across the grain and arrange on a bed of lettuce.

To make Tonnato Sauce, place drained tuna in a bowl with mayonnaise, chopped capers, lemon juice and pepper. Add 1-2 tbsp water, as needed, and mix with a fork to a creamy consistency or purée for a smoother sauce, adding a little more mayonnaise if required.

To serve, spoon tuna onto sliced chicken breasts and garnish with sprigs of thyme and chopped olives.

Red Duck Curry

This quick curry gets its richness from the coconut cream and cashews. Asian supermarkets frequently sell hot barbecued ducks – for a quick meal, pick one up on the way home and ask the duck man to chop it up for you, leaving the meat on the bone. If you can't get duck just use chicken.

Prep time   10 mins
Cook time   15 mins
Serves   2

2 spring onions

1 tbsp neutral oil

2-3 tbsp red curry paste

500ml chicken stock

1 cup coconut cream

2 tsp fish sauce

finely grated zest of 1 lime

½ tsp soft brown sugar

1 medium tomato,
cored and diced

½ barbecued duck,
cut in chunks

2 handfuls (100g) green
beans, trimmed

2 tbsp toasted cashews,
very finely chopped

To serve
coriander leaves (optional)

cooked basmati rice

Finely chop spring onions, reserving green part to add at the end. Heat oil in a medium pot and fry red curry paste and white part of spring onions for about 30 seconds. Add chicken stock, coconut cream, fish sauce, lime zest, sugar, tomato and duck and simmer 10 minutes.

When ready to serve, add beans and cashews and cook until beans are just tender (about 5 minutes).

To serve, stir in reserved green part of spring onions. Garnish with coriander leaves, if using, and serve with rice.

Spicy Duck Bowl

Here's another great idea for a special but speedy meal made from a store-bought barbecued duck. Buy a whole duck, remove the breast meat and save the rest for a Red Duck Curry (see page 143) or Duck and Mango Salad (see page 72).

Prep time   20 mins
Cook time   15 mins
Serves   4

2 cooked duck breasts

300g dried udon noodles

2 litres chicken stock

1 tbsp grated fresh ginger

finely grated zest of ½ orange

¼ cup soy sauce

2 tbsp fish sauce

2 red chillies, deseeded
and thinly sliced

8 button mushrooms,
thinly sliced

100g broccolini or broccoli,
cut into florets (optional)

3 heads bok choy, quartered,

4 spring onions, finely sliced

Slice duck very thinly. Cook noodles according to packet instructions, then rinse and drain.

Place chicken stock in a large pot with ginger, orange zest, soy sauce and fish sauce. Simmer 10 minutes. Add red chillies, button mushrooms and broccolini or broccoli, if using. Simmer until the vegetables are just tender (about 3 minutes).

Just before serving, add duck, bok choy and spring onions and stir over medium heat until bok choy is wilted (about 2 minutes). Run boiling water over noodles to loosen and heat through. Drain noodles and divide between serving bowls. Top with duck, vegetables and broth and serve immediately.

Refreshing Fruit Combos

During the week a bowl of fresh fruit on the table usually suffices as dessert in our house, but if you fancy something a bit more exciting try these easy combinations, which make the most of whatever fresh fruit is in season.

Strawberries in Balsamic

Hull 2 punnets (about 500g) strawberries and slice in half vertically. Place ½ cup sugar and 2 tbsp water in a small pot and cook over medium heat, swirling the pot occasionally, until sugar melts and begins to caramelise. Stir in 1 tbsp balsamic vinegar and drizzle over the top of the strawberries. Leave to macerate for 10 minutes. Serve topped with a dollop of crème fraiche.

Caramel Oranges and Kiwifruit

Peel 6 oranges, removing all pith. Cut the flesh into segments or thin slices and place in a serving bowl with 6 peeled and angle-sliced kiwifruit. Place 1 cup sugar and ¼ cup water in a small pot over medium heat, swirling the pot occasionally, until sugar has dissolved. Increase heat and boil until mixture forms a rich golden caramel. Pour at once over fruit. Stand 1-2 hours before serving. Just before serving, pour 2-3 tbsp Grand Marnier or Cointreau (optional) over fruit. Serve with vanilla ice cream. Serves 6.

Mixed Berry Salad

Place a punnet (about 120g) each of fresh raspberries and blueberries in a serving bowl with 2 tbsp unsalted raw pistachios. To make a sauce, mix 1 tbsp raspberry jam with 2 tbsp fresh orange juice. Drizzle sauce over fruit and nuts. Serves 2-4.

Even in the
routine of
everyday
life, there is
pleasure
to be found
in the simplest
things. Taking
the time to
enjoy special
moments
creates
feel-good
memories
for life.

Ginger Peach Parfait

I love this easy throw-together take on the gingernut cream log that was all the rage in the 1960s. It's so simple to layer up for a last-minute after-dinner treat. I like to make individual servings in glass tumblers, but you could make it as one big trifle. For a family-friendly version, use orange juice in place of the sherry.

Prep time	10 mins
	+ soaking
Serves	4

8 gingernut biscuits

¼ cup sherry

400g can peach slices in syrup

300ml cream

1 tsp vanilla extract

1 tsp finely grated fresh ginger

1 tbsp icing sugar

¼ cup orange juice

Break 7 gingernuts into 8-10 pieces each and place in a shallow bowl. Pour the sherry over the top and leave to stand while you prepare the rest of the dessert.

Place remaining gingernut in a paper bag and whack with a rolling pin to make rough crumbs. Place to one side.

Drain peaches, reserving syrup. In a separate bowl, whip cream to soft peaks with vanilla, ginger and icing sugar. Tip in the soaked gingernuts and any remaining soaking liquid, add the reserved peach syrup and orange juice and fold together. Mixture should be loose and silky.

Divide three quarters of the peaches between 4 parfait glasses and spoon two thirds of the cream mixture over the top. Add the rest of the peaches then spoon over the remaining cream mixture. Sprinkle gingernut crumbs over the top and serve. If not serving at once, Ginger Peach Parfaits can be kept in the fridge for up to an hour before serving.

Cheats' Gourmet Ice Cream

Make your own gourmet ice cream by stirring your favourite flavourings through inexpensive vanilla ice cream. Inspired by some timeless sweet treats, these light-hearted combinations will bring out the sweet tooth in everyone.

Peanut Butter and Jelly Ice Cream

Make up 2 packets of cherry or berry jelly according to packet instructions but using half the amount of water. Refrigerate until cool but not set, stirring occasionally. Remove 2 litres vanilla ice cream from the freezer and allow it to soften without melting (20-30 minutes). Empty into a large bowl, reserving 3 tbsp in the container and stirring 4 tbsp peanut butter through it. Mix into the rest of the ice cream, then swirl in jelly. Return to freezer to set, using a second container if necessary to hold the extra volume. About 10 minutes before serving remove from freezer to soften.

Coconut Ice Swirl

Remove 2 litres vanilla ice cream from the freezer and allow it to soften without melting (20-30 minutes). Lightly toast 2 cups thread coconut and allow to cool. Empty ice cream into a large bowl and stir through the coconut. Thaw 2 cups frozen berries, mix with 1 cup raspberry or strawberry jam then swirl through ice cream. Return to freezer to set, using a second container if necessary to hold the extra volume. About 10 minutes before serving remove from freezer to soften.

Jaffa Ice

Remove 2 litres vanilla ice cream from the freezer and allow it to soften without melting (20-30 minutes). Stir in 4 tbsp fresh orange juice or Cointreau or Grand Marnier. Roughly chop 100g Jaffas or dark chocolate and fold through, using a second container if necessary to hold the extra volume. Return to freezer to set. About 10 minutes before serving remove from freezer to soften.

Rocky Road Ice Cream

Remove 2 litres vanilla ice cream from the freezer and allow it to soften without melting (about 20-30 minutes). Empty into a large bowl. Stir in 4 crumbled meringues, 2 cups marshmallow bits and 1 cup roughly chopped scorched almonds. Return to freezer to set, using a second container if necessary to hold the extra volume. About 10 minutes before serving remove from freezer to soften.

Asian Flavours for Unexpected Guests

If friends turn up unannounced I'll just add an extra course or two to our family meal – defrosting prawns for a salad and whipping dessert out of the freezer.

A bowl of wasabi peas or spiced nuts

∾

Spring Prawn Salad, page 52

∾

Ginger Chilli Sweet and Sour Chicken, page 134

Lightly cooked greens

Jasmine rice

∾

Jaffa Ice, page 152

∾

Chilled dry riesling

Retro Dinner in a Rush

Food is like fashion. Timeless classics may go out of favour for a while, but they always come back, delivering a sense of nostalgia with a modern twist.

Oysters with Kilpatrick Topping, page 261

Chicken Tonnato, page 140

French bread

Ginger Peach Parfait, page 151

Chilled sauvignon blanc

For prep plans, shopping lists and more menus
see annabel-langbein.com

barbecues

Everything tastes better when it's cooked outdoors.

When you eat outdoors there's a sense that you're on holiday – a feel-good factor that extends summer beyond its meagre calendar allotment. The informality of cooking over an open flame loosens everyone up, and there are never any expectations of gourmandism (at least not within my friends and family).

Barbecuing is such a relaxing way to enjoy the company of friends, whether you're welcoming them into your home or meeting them for an evening picnic at the beach. The traditional antipodean barbie – where everybody brings a salad and something to throw on the grill – is a stress-free formula for feeding a crowd.

At home we barbecue at any opportunity. If it's just for two or three of us, I'll grill some meat, chicken or fish and toss it through seasonal salad fixings and a tasty dressing as a simple one-dish dinner. If friends with small children are coming over, I'll make sure I pick up some sausages from my local butcher, along with a loaf of fresh white bread to wrap them in with a squirt of tomato sauce.

The things that make barbecues interesting are the marinades and rubs you use on meats or fish, and the dressings you use on salads or thrown-together combinations of char-grilled vegetables. To make a great sauce to serve on the side, save a little unused marinade to mix with sour cream, mayo or puréed mangos or peaches and chopped fresh herbs. It echoes the barbecue flavours in a very harmonious way.

You can take a mix-and-match approach with marinades – most work equally well with meats, seafoods and vegetables – but aim to stick with one style of cuisine rather than leapfrogging around the globe. It's much more satisfying to eat within one family of flavours than a hotchpotch of east and west and everything in between.

Barbecued Vege Combos

Use these ideas as side dishes with grilled meats or fish, or make several for a tapas-style vegetarian meal. They can be served warm or at room temperature.

Grilled Veges with Sesame Sauce

To make Sesame Sauce, stir together 2 tbsp tahini, 2 tbsp water, 1 tsp grated fresh ginger, 1 tbsp lemon juice and ½ tsp soy sauce. Halve 3 long asian eggplants lengthwise and trim 2 bunches asparagus. Brush with olive oil, season and grill over medium-low heat until softened and lightly browned (asparagus takes about 8 minutes and eggplant 5-6 minutes each side). Arrange on a platter and top with Sesame Sauce and 2 tsp toasted sesame seeds. Serves 4 as a side dish.

Mediterranean Vegetable Toss

Cut 1 eggplant in half lengthwise, then into finger-wide slices. Core 2 red peppers and cut into 8-10 pieces. Brush eggplant and peppers with olive oil, season and barbecue until tender (5-6 minutes each side). Place in a bowl with 6 small tomatoes, cored and halved, 2 handfuls basil, 2 handfuls rocket and 100g crumbled feta. Toss with 2 tbsp Parsley Pesto (see page 254) or store-bought pesto and 2 tbsp boutique extra virgin olive oil, season to taste and serve. Serves 4-6 as a side dish.

Barbecue Lemon Garlic Mushrooms

In a small pot sizzle 50g butter, 2 crushed cloves garlic and 1 tsp fresh thyme for 1 minute. Remove from heat and add 1 tbsp lemon juice. Trim stems of 12-15 flat mushrooms. Lightly brush or spray with olive oil and grill skin-side up for 2 minutes. Turn over, top each with 1 tsp garlic butter, season and grill over low heat until cooked through (about 8-10 minutes). Serves 4 as a side dish.

Char-Grilled Red and Yellow Peppers

Halve and deseed 6 large red or yellow peppers. Place skin-side down on a heated barbecue and grill until the skins are charred (about 10 minutes). Place on a plate, cover until cool enough to handle, then remove skins and slice flesh into thin strips. Arrange in piles on a plate, drizzle with boutique extra virgin olive oil and sprinkle with salt, pepper and 1 tsp finely chopped capers. Serves 4 as a side dish. Also great as part of an antipasti platter or as a topping for bruschetta.

Shopping with your senses

My mother cultivated an astute relationship with Cyril, her butcher. Meat was the biggest expense in her budget and she charmingly ensured that we always got the best.
If something was a little tough or not quite up to par she would point it out to Cyril, keeping him on his toes.

Cooking well starts when you shop: seeking out the heaviest, most fragrant, unblemished melon; the fattest fish, which smells only of the sea, with glistening eyes and bright red gills, firm and bouncy to the touch; a piece of beautifully aged beef that does not bounce back but gives gently and is not glistening blood-red but rather a dull, dark-ruby hue, with a dry brown edge where the air has aged it; nuts that smell like… well… nuts – a rich, milky, sweetmeat aroma and nary a hint of sour rancidity. These are the clues to freshness and quality that make your work in the kitchen easy.

The fish that looks dull and flabby, with sad grey eyes, brownish-red gills and that decidedly fishy smell, is to be avoided. Every hour at room temperature equates to a day's shelf life for fresh fish, whereas gutted and kept very cold it will last for up to 12 days.

Chicken quality can be determined in part by size. Huge, luminous white chicken breasts signal birds reared in cages and fed on a super-sizing diet that renders them ready for the table in just six weeks. By comparison, free-range chickens that have grown slowly and naturally without antibiotics have smaller breasts, denser, darker flesh and more flavour.

Selecting fresh ingredients engages all your senses. Learn to distinguish the fragrance of ripeness versus that slightly fermented smell when something is over-ripe, or the whiff of no return. Slimy texture points to protein that is no longer fresh and may need to be thrown out. When it comes to produce, pick it up, eyeball it, roll it gently in your hand, smell it and make your call.

The moment when something is so astonishingly delectable, so extraordinarily delicious that you lose yourself in the sheer marvel of taste, texture and smell, is an epiphany. Nothing will ever taste quite the same. You will seek it out again, perhaps finding it in a sun-kissed white peach or a sweet, warm, vine-ripened tomato. Nature's best offerings convert our taste forever.

BLUFF OYSTERS IN STORE

Scallops with Lemon Caper Butter

These dead-simple scallops are delicious with a chilled riesling. You'll need 15-18 cleaned scallop shells (the curved half). These can be washed and kept to use again next time. If you're not feeling that flush, use half scallops and half skinless, boneless white fish fillets that have been cut into scallop-sized chunks.

Prep time   5 mins
Cook time   3 mins
Serves   6-8

30-36 scallops

salt and ground black pepper

Lemon Caper Butter
100g butter

1 tbsp capers, finely chopped

finely grated zest of 1 lemon

10-12 basil leaves,
finely chopped

2 tbsp finely grated parmesan

To make Lemon Caper Butter, heat the butter in a microwave or small pot until it is just melted. Mix in the capers, lemon zest, basil and parmesan.

Place 2 scallops in each of 15-18 cleaned scallop shells and top each shell with a heaped tsp lemon caper butter. Season with salt and pepper to taste. The scallops can be prepared ahead until this point and stored covered in the fridge for up to 4 hours until needed.

When ready to serve, place scallops in their shells on a heated barbecue. Cook over a high heat until butter bubbles (about 2 minutes), then turn scallops in butter and cook another minute. Do not overcook – they need to be opaque but still slightly rare so they don't shrink and get tough. Serve immediately.

Snapper with Black Bean Sauce

Umami (loosely translated as savoury deliciousness) has quite recently been identified as the fifth taste, alongside sweet, sour, salty and bitter. Black bean sauce gives this dish that wonderful depth of flavour. If you don't have black bean sauce, follow the method with miso or oyster sauce, also rich in umami.

Prep time   5 mins
Cook time   20 mins
Serves   4

2 tbsp black bean sauce

2 tbsp grated fresh ginger

1 tsp sesame oil

1 tsp sugar

juice of 1 lime or lemon

1 cleaned and scaled snapper or other white fish (about 1.2kg gutted weight)

Broccolini Cashew Toss
2 bunches broccolini
or 1 large head of broccoli cut into florets

½ cup water

1 tbsp neutral oil

1 tsp fish sauce

½ cup toasted cashews or almonds

To garnish
2 spring onions,
cut into long, thin strips

slices of lime

Place black bean sauce, ginger, sesame oil, sugar and lime or lemon juice in a bowl and mix to combine.

Layer two large sheets of tin foil on the bench. Place snapper in the centre and cut 3-4 deep slashes in each side. Rub black bean mixture over both sides of fish, rubbing into cavity and gashes. Wrap up tin foil tightly to seal. The snapper can be prepared to this stage and cooked immediately or chilled for up to 8 hours before cooking.

When ready to cook, place fish in its tin foil parcel onto a preheated barbecue and cook over medium heat for 20 minutes, or preheat oven to 200°C and bake fish for 20 minutes or until flesh gives without resistance when a wooden skewer is passed through the foil just behind the gills. The eye should also be starting to whiten.

While the fish is cooking, prepare the Broccolini Cashew Toss. Place broccolini or broccoli in a pot with water, neutral oil and fish sauce. Cover and cook until just tender (about 5 minutes). Toss with toasted cashews or almonds.

Place Broccolini Cashew Toss on a serving platter with the fish and spoon over the fish cooking juices. Garnish with spring onions and slices of lime and serve immediately.

Barbecued Sticks and Skewers

Break the ice at a barbecue by getting everyone to cook their own meat, chicken or fish on skewers. It's such a sociable way to cook. Mix and match meats or seafoods with marinades of your choice and soak wooden skewers or disposable chopsticks in water for half an hour before use to reduce burning.

Thai Chicken Kebabs

Cut 2 single skinless chicken breasts into 10cm x 2cm strips and place in a bowl with ¼ cup thai sweet chilli sauce, 1 tbsp fish sauce and 2 tbsp lime juice. Toss to coat evenly and marinate for at least 20 minutes or up to 4 hours in the fridge. Push skewers up the length of the chicken strips. Barbecue over medium heat until cooked through (about 5 minutes each side). Drizzle with the juice of 1 lime and serve on Market Noodle Salad (see page 62). Makes about 12 skewers. Serves 4.

Lemon Chicken Skewers with Spiked Yoghurt Sauce

Cut 2 single skinless chicken breasts on the diagonal into finger-thick slices. Place in a bowl with the juice of 1 lemon, 1 tbsp olive oil, 2 tsp rosemary leaves, salt and pepper and toss to coat. Thread onto skewers. To make Spiked Yoghurt Sauce, stir together 1 cup greek yoghurt, ½ cup mayonnaise, the finely grated zest and juice of 2 limes, 1 tbsp fish sauce, 1 tsp sugar, 1 crushed clove garlic, 2 tsp grated fresh ginger, 1 tsp turmeric, ¼ cup chopped coriander and about 1 tsp very finely chopped red chilli, to taste. Barbecue chicken over medium heat for 5 minutes each side or until cooked through. Serve with Spiked Yoghurt Sauce. Any remaining sauce will keep in the fridge for several days for later use with seafood, pork or vegetables. Makes about 12 skewers. Serves 4.

Tandoori Fish Kebabs

Cut 500g boneless, skinless firm white fish fillets into 2-3cm chunks and mix in a bowl with 2 tbsp store-bought tandoori marinade and ½ cup greek yoghurt. Cover and set aside for 15 minutes or up to 2 hours in the fridge. To make kebabs, thread fish onto chopsticks and season. Lightly oil a barbecue hotplate and cook over medium-high heat until cooked through (about 2-3 minutes each side). Serve with rice and Cucumber and Yoghurt Salad (see page 223). Serves 4.

Even in the middle of the city and the middle of the week, a barbecue at the beach creates a summer-holiday moment.

Mediterranean Lamb Salad

This salad brings together my favourite high-summer flavours. Tuna steaks are a delicious alternative to lamb, or use extra eggplant for a vegetarian version.

Prep time   20 mins
               + marinating
Cook time   15 mins
Serves   6

8 lamb fillets

2 tsp chopped rosemary

finely grated zest of 1 lemon

2 cloves garlic, crushed

1 tbsp olive oil

salt and ground black pepper

6 tomatoes

4 roasted peppers, peeled and sliced into strips

1 cup kalamata olives

1 large bunch basil leaves

¼ cup caperberries

¼ cup semi-dried tomatoes, thinly sliced

2 smallish long asian eggplants

Basic Vinaigrette
3 tbsp lemon juice

½ cup olive oil

½ tsp mustard

½ tsp sugar

1 clove garlic, crushed

salt and ground black pepper

To make marinade for the lamb, combine rosemary, lemon zest, garlic, olive oil and salt and pepper to taste. Mix through lamb and marinate for at least 15 minutes or up to 4 hours in the fridge.

While lamb is marinating, prepare the salad. Core tomatoes, cut into wedges and place in a serving bowl with roasted peppers, olives, basil, caperberries and semi-dried tomatoes.

To make the Basic Vinaigrette, combine lemon juice, olive oil, mustard, sugar, garlic and salt and pepper to taste in a small jar and shake until combined.

Angle-slice eggplants into finger-wide slices. Brush or spray with a little oil and barbecue over medium heat until golden brown (about 5-6 minutes each side). Stack on a plate and cover with a clean teatowel so they steam and soften further as they cool.

Barbecue lamb over high heat until done to your liking (about 2-3 minutes each side for medium-rare). Set aside to rest for at least 5 minutes.

When ready to serve, cut lamb into finger-wide strips on the diagonal. Add to salad with eggplant and Basic Vinaigrette and toss gently to combine. Any remaining vinaigrette can be stored in the fridge for later use. It will last for several weeks.

Prep-Ahead Grill-and-Toss Salads

Take the stress out of entertaining with one-dish meals. Marinate your meat or seafood in advance, then simply sear it on the barbecue and toss with salad to serve.

Spicy Squid and Grapefruit Salad

Criss-cross score the underside of 500g baby squid or squid tubes and cut into 5cm x 3cm pieces. Mix through 1 tbsp soft brown sugar, 1 tbsp fish sauce, 2 tbsp lime juice, 2 crushed cloves garlic and 1 finely chopped red chilli and marinate 20-30 minutes in the fridge. To make Asian Chilli Dressing, shake in a small jar 2 tbsp lime juice, 1 tbsp fish sauce and 1 tbsp thai sweet chilli sauce. To make salad, toss 2 peeled, segmented grapefruit, 2 sliced avocados and 8 handfuls (200g) rocket or watercress. Heat barbecue hot plate with a little olive oil and sear squid over high heat until colour changes (about 1 minute each side). Add to salad with Asian Chilli Dressing and toss. Serves 6.

Barbecued Chicken Chickpea Toss

Split 2 single chicken breasts horizontally and pound to even thickness. Marinate with juice of 1 lemon, 1 tsp chopped rosemary, 1 tsp thyme leaves and salt and pepper for 15 minutes or up to 2 hours in the fridge. Cut 2 medium red onions into thin wedges and soften in olive oil over low heat for 5 minutes. Boil ½ head cauliflower florets until just tender, adding 150g spinach for the last 20 seconds to wilt. Drain. Angle-slice 2 spring onions and 2 stalks celery and toss with onions, cauliflower, spinach, 2 tbsp chopped coriander and a 400g can chickpeas, drained and rinsed. Barbecue chicken until cooked through (4-5 minutes each side). Rest 5 minutes, angle-slice and add to salad with ⅓ cup Curry Mayo (see page 254). Toss, adjust seasonings and serve. Serves 4.

Grilled Lamb with Spring Burghul Salad

Mix 6-8 lamb fillets, 2 tbsp chopped mint, 2 tbsp tapenade, 2 crushed cloves garlic and 3 tbsp lemon juice and marinate 15 minutes or up to 4 hours in the fridge. Prepare 2 cups burghul wheat or israeli couscous according to packet instructions. Pour boiling water over 12 sliced asparagus spears or beans, stand 2 minutes, drain, then add to drained burghul or couscous with ¼ cup lemon juice, 2 tbsp olive oil, ⅔ cup chopped mint or parsley, ¼ cup toasted pine nuts, 2 tbsp finely chopped preserved lemon (optional) and salt and pepper to taste. Heat barbecue with a little olive oil and cook lamb over high heat until done to your liking (about 2-3 minutes each side for medium-rare). Rest 5 minutes, angle-slice then toss through salad and serve with pita bread. Serves 6.

Grilled Flank Steak with Quick Green Sauce

Flank steak isn't the tenderest of beef cuts, but it has great flavour so it's perfect for cooking on the barbecue and serving with a gutsy sauce and a selection of salads – for salad ideas see pages 160, 184 and 280. This Quick Green Sauce is also delicious in Tuna Niçoise on Turkish Flatbread (see page 23).

Prep time	5 mins
Cook time	10-14 mins
	+ resting
Serves	4-6

600-800g piece of flank steak

olive oil, for grilling

salt and ground black pepper

Quick Green Sauce
1 tightly packed cup rocket
or watercress leaves

green tops of 1 spring onion
or a small bunch of chives

2 tsp capers

⅓ cup olive oil

salt and ground black pepper

Rub the steak with a little olive oil and season with salt and pepper to taste. Heat the barbecue and cook steak over a high heat until done to your liking (about 5-7 minutes each side for medium-rare). Rest for 10 minutes.

To make Quick Green Sauce, place rocket or watercress leaves, spring onions or chives, capers, olive oil and salt and pepper to taste in a food processor and purée to form a smooth, vibrantly green sauce.

When ready to serve, thinly angle-slice the steak across the grain. Serve with Quick Green Sauce on the side. Any remaining sauce can be kept in a jar in the fridge for up to a week.

Help-yourself Hot Steak Sandwiches

These sandwiches are a stylish alternative to burgers at a casual barbecue and an easy meal option when cooking for one or two. You could also offer roasted red peppers, grilled mushrooms, marinated artichokes, slices of avocado, onion jam, pesto, salsa, blue cheese or whatever other fillings take your fancy.

Prep time	5 mins
Cook time	4-6 mins
Serves	4

4 medium steaks,
such as sirloin

olive oil, for grilling

salt and ground black pepper

8 thick slices sourdough
or five-grain bread

4 tbsp aioli or mayonnaise

4 tbsp spicy tomato relish

4 small handfuls (100g)
rocket leaves

4 medium tomatoes

Rub the steaks with a little olive oil and season with salt and pepper to taste. Heat the barbecue and cook steak over a high heat until done to your liking (about 2-3 minutes each side for medium-rare). Remove from heat to rest while preparing the other ingredients.

Place bread slices on the heated grill and weight down with a heatproof plate for a few seconds to press the bread onto the grill bars and create char marks. Turn bread and repeat. Spread 4 slices of toasted bread with tomato relish and the other 4 slices with aioli or mayonnaise.

Slice steak on the diagonal into finger-thick strips. Place everything on the table and invite everyone to help themselves, piling steak onto the grilled bread slices spread with tomato relish, then topping with a handful of rocket leaves, then tomato slices and finally the slices of toasted bread spread with aioli or mayonnaise.

Develop your own free-range style

Recipes are like road maps. They should guide you easily from your starting point (the ingredients at hand) to your destination (the delicious dish on the table) with no crashes, potholes, detours or wrong turns on the way. Apart from baking, which is pure chemistry, cooking is not an exact science. Ovens vary in temperature and ingredients differ in their age and quality. When things go wrong, as they will now and then, you tend not to think "what a useless recipe" but "I've failed", and your confidence plummets.

Learning to cook is a bit like learning to drive in a new city. Not only do you have no idea where you are going or what landmarks to look out for, you also have no idea of the mechanics. Gradually you learn and start to feel a rhythm in your cooking, trusting your instincts and your taste. In this way, through trial and error and tasting, tasting, tasting, you start to develop your own cooking style.

The good cooks I know all share a natural warmth and generosity of spirit, an innate resourcefulness and an easy confidence around food. Give them a kitchen and a handful of ingredients and in next to no time, with little fuss or effort, they will produce something appetising and original – no recipe needed. Reaching this point takes time and confidence because cooking, just like any other craft, is a skill and the more you do, the better you will become.

When you start cooking you are a slave to the recipe in front of you, but after you have made a dish once or twice you'll have the confidence to take shortcuts, adapt and improvise to suit your own tastes. I happen to like chilli and coriander. Perhaps you don't, so you may choose to substitute other flavours such as ginger and lime or mint or perhaps star anise.

As you develop your own cooking style, you will become more intuitive and creative. The more you taste, the more refined your flavour memory becomes and this is what you will draw on when you start to adapt recipes and create your own dishes. Learning from the things that went wrong and being adventurous provides a freedom that gives great pleasure in the kitchen. It's what defines my free-range cooking style. Be the master of your own palate, be curious, take joy in what nature provides and prepare food that makes your tastebuds sing.

For more kitchen know-how see annabel-langbein.com

Sticky Chilli Ribs with Pineapple Salsa

This finger-licking recipe is a winner with adults and children alike, although you may like to tone down the chilli if you're cooking it for kids. There's something about eating with your fingers that makes food taste better.

Prep time	15 mins
	+ marinating
Cook time	30-40 mins
Serves	6-8

about 2-2.5kg short pork ribs

½ cup thai sweet chilli sauce

finely grated zest of 2 limes

2 tbsp grated or finely chopped lemongrass

1 tbsp soy sauce

1 tbsp fish sauce

2 red chillies, deseeded and finely chopped (optional)

Pineapple Salsa
½ pineapple, peeled, cored and finely diced

2 red chillies, deseeded and very finely chopped

20 mint leaves, finely shredded

2 tbsp lime juice

salt and ground black pepper

Grilled Kumara
3 kumara, peeled

olive oil, for brushing

Cut pork racks into pieces with about 8 ribs in each piece. Place in a bowl with thai sweet chilli sauce, lime zest, lemongrass, soy sauce, fish sauce and chillies and marinate in the fridge for at least 30 minutes or overnight.

To make the Pineapple Salsa, mix together pineapple, chillies, mint, lime juice, salt and pepper. Pineapple Salsa can be made in advance and will keep in the fridge for 1-2 days.

When ready to serve, lift pork out of marinade and barbecue over a medium heat until golden and cooked through (about 15-20 minutes each side), or place in a single layer in a large, shallow roasting dish with 2 cups water and roast in a 200°C oven until cooked through and golden brown (about 1 hour). You will know it is cooked if the juices run clear when a skewer is inserted into the thickest part. Set aside to rest.

To prepare Grilled Kumara, cut kumara into finger-thick slices and criss-cross score on both sides. Brush with oil, season with salt and pepper and grill over medium heat until tender (about 6-8 minutes each side).

Cut pork into individual ribs and serve with Grilled Kumara and Pineapple Salsa on the side.

Portable Salads for Barbecues and Picnics

Kiwi tradition demands that you turn up for a barbecue with something to throw on the grill and a salad to add to the communal meal. These carb-based salads all transport well, so they're also perfect for lunchboxes and picnics.

Roasted Vegetable Orzo with Pomegranate Vinaigrette

Soak ½ cup currants in ¼ cup orange juice. Peel and dice 600g pumpkin and 600g beetroot, place on a lined roasting tray and drizzle with 2 tbsp olive oil and 2 tbsp maple syrup. Season and bake at 200°C until tender (about 30 minutes), adding 1 cup walnut pieces in the last 10 minutes to toast. Cool. Cook 500g orzo for 1 minute less than specified in packet instructions (to give a firmer texture). To make Pomegranate Vinaigrette, mix 2 tbsp olive oil, 3 crushed cloves garlic, 2 tbsp pomegranate molasses, 1 tbsp rice vinegar and 2 tbsp lemon juice. Drain orzo, place in a large bowl, add Pomegranate Vinaigrette, currants and juice, and toss immediately. Just before serving, toss in pumpkin, beetroot, walnuts and ½ cup chopped coriander or parsley. Serves 8-10 as a side dish.

Purple Wheat Salad

Place 1½ cups purple wheat in a pot and cover with boiling water. Cover with a lid and boil until tender (about 1 hour), topping up water as needed. Drain. Mix in 1 tsp cumin, the finely grated zest of 1 lemon, 2 tbsp olive oil, 2 crushed cloves garlic, 3 tbsp lemon juice and ½ cup chopped dried cranberries. Season to taste with salt and pepper. When cool, mix in 2 tbsp chopped coriander, 2 tbsp chopped mint and ½ cup chopped pistachios. Serves 6 as a side dish.

Quinoa Salad with Tomatoes and Herby Dressing

Toast 1 cup dry red or white quinoa in a pan until it starts to smell nutty and begins to pop (about 2-3 minutes). Place in a sieve and rinse under cold water until water runs clear. Place in a pot with 3 cups water, bring to a boil then cover and simmer until grains have become transparent, the spiral-like germ has separated and water has been absorbed (about 15 minutes). Cool. To make Herby Dressing, shake in a jar 2 crushed cloves garlic, ½ cup finely chopped basil or mint, 1 tbsp lemon juice, 1 tsp rice vinegar, 3 tbsp olive oil, 1 tsp finely crushed toasted coriander seeds, and salt and pepper to taste. Core and chop 3 medium tomatoes and stir into quinoa with 2 cups edamame beans or sweetcorn kernels, 2 handfuls baby spinach and Herby Dressing. Serves 6-8 as a side dish.

Weekend Barbecue

Everyone loves the conviviality of a casual weekend barbecue. It's such a low-stress way to gather a bunch of friends together.

Crudité with Curry Mayo
and Balsamic Oil Dips, page 254

Smoked Salmon au Naturel, page 254

∾

Sticky Chilli Ribs with Pineapple Salsa, page 182

Grilled Kumara, page 182

Quinoa Salad with Tomatoes and
Herby Dressing, page 184

∾

Strawberry Limoncello Tiramisu, page 292

∾

Chilled beer

Seafood on the Grill

This seafood feast is the perfect menu to celebrate a successful day out fishing – or just the fact that it's a summer's day in the city.

🍴

Spicy Squid and Grapefruit Salad, page 174

෴

Snapper with Black Bean Sauce, page 166

Broccolini Cashew Toss, page 166

Japanese-Style Rice, page 122

෴

Pistachio Praline Semifreddo, page 229

෴

Chilled pinot gris

For prep plans, shopping lists and more menus
see annabel-langbein.com

make-ahead meals

*When everything's organised
you can relax and have fun.*

Some 20 years ago my dear friend Daniele Delpeuch, once the private cook of President Mitterrand, made a trip out from France to visit us. I was keen to show her some local hospitality, so I invited ten foodie people to join us for what was supposed to be a glamorous and impressive midweek dinner.

Around 6.30pm I arrived home from work feeling frazzled. For some reason I didn't have a thing prepared and I had no clear plan of what we would eat. Winging it was my style and I loved the adrenaline buzz – that's youth for you.

But this time something wasn't jelling. I had thought a leg of wild pork would be a fabulous main but had failed to take it out of the freezer. The first wave of panic hit as I realised there was no way to fast-thaw it and the butcher and supermarket were closed. Tout fermé. I rattled around in the freezer and found a lonely lamb rack. Ten people, one lamb rack – the maths wasn't looking good.

I made a savoury fruit sauce, but it was so disgusting it got the biff. Bang, bang, bang like a line of dominoes, each idea crashed on its face. I have no recall of what we did eat in the end – probably half a lamb chop each and some cheese. Luckily one of the guests brought some remarkable wines and we all got plastered!

In the morning Daniele gently enquired whether I was okay. "Perhaps, ma petite, you are working too hard?" It was a relief, some weeks later, to call her with the news that I was newly pregnant. My head had obviously done an early dip into the nappy bucket. From that point on, I pretty well gave up the winging it strategy. Now I give thought to my menu in advance, choosing flavours that go together while providing a balance of rich and light, and making sure I include some dishes I can prepare in advance to pull out of the fridge or freezer. Voilà – c'est tout organisé!

Spinach Ricotta Gnocchi with Walnut Butter

Make these light-as-air ricotta dumplings ahead of time, then fire them into a hot oven for a few minutes just before serving. You could top them with a tomato sauce or a blue cheese sauce made by melting 50g blue cheese with 1 cup cream, but I like this simple Walnut Butter. Serve with a crisp green salad.

Prep time	30 mins
Cook time	6-10 mins
Serves	4-6 as a starter
	or 3 as a main

400g ricotta

2 eggs

1 egg yolk

½ packed cup cooked spinach, all water squeezed out, chopped finely

2 tbsp finely grated parmesan

½ tsp freshly grated nutmeg

finely grated zest of 1 lemon

½ tsp salt

ground black pepper

¼ cup flour, plus extra for dusting

Walnut Butter
3 tbsp butter

½ cup roughly chopped walnuts

1 tsp finely chopped thyme leaves

Combine ricotta, eggs, yolk, spinach, parmesan, nutmeg, lemon zest, salt, pepper and flour. Stir until evenly mixed (the mixture will be quite wet).

Bring a 3-litre pot of salted water to a boil. Use a teaspoon to shape walnut-sized balls of ricotta mixture (makes about 36), dropping them onto a plate of flour and tossing gently to coat.

Working in batches of 5-6 at a time so as not to overcrowd the pot, shake any excess flour from the gnocchi then drop them into the boiling water. Simmer gently until they rise to the surface (about 2-3 minutes). Once risen, allow to simmer for a further minute then lift out with a slotted spoon and place in a lightly greased baking dish. If not serving immediately, cover and refrigerate for up to 24 hours. To freeze, drain boiled gnocchi on paper towels, transfer to a tray and freeze. Bring back to room temperature before baking.

When ready to serve, preheat oven to 200°C.

To make the Walnut Butter, place butter, walnuts and thyme in a small pot and cook over a medium heat for 2-3 minutes until walnuts are golden.

Pour over the dumplings and place in oven until sizzling (about 6-10 minutes). Serve immediately.

Feta Polenta Wedges with Roast Veges

Your vegetarian friends will feel spoilt when you serve up this satisfying meal, but it is also good served as an accompaniment to roast lamb or beef. It's a useful recipe to adapt with whatever vegetables are in season.

Prep time	20 mins
Cook time	60 mins
Serves	4

Feta Polenta Wedges
3½ cups water

¾ tsp salt

ground black pepper

1 cup instant polenta, plus extra for coating

1 tbsp butter

100g feta, crumbled

¼ tsp ground nutmeg

½ tsp finely chopped rosemary

2 tbsp olive oil, for frying

Roast Veges
2 red onions, peeled

2 red peppers, deseeded

6 zucchini, halved lengthwise

4 tbsp olive oil

finely grated zest of ½ a lemon

8 tomatoes, cored and halved

4-8 flat mushrooms

12 cloves garlic, unpeeled

To serve
½ cup pesto

To make the Feta Polenta Wedges, line a dish measuring about 20cm x 25cm with baking paper.

Bring water, salt and pepper to a boil in a medium pot. Add polenta in a thin stream as you stir. Cover and cook over a low heat for 3 minutes. The mixture will be very thick (take care when you lift the lid as it splatters). Stir in butter, feta, nutmeg and rosemary until evenly combined. Pour polenta into prepared dish, spread evenly and chill at least 2 hours until firm. It will keep in the fridge for up to 48 hours.

To roast the vegetables, preheat oven to 170°C. Line a roasting dish with baking paper. Halve onions then cut each half into 4-6 wedges. Cut each red pepper into 8 pieces and add to the dish with onions and zucchini. Drizzle with 2 tbsp olive oil and lemon zest, toss to coat and season with salt and pepper. Spread out to a single layer. Roast until starting to soften (about 20 minutes). Add tomatoes, mushrooms and garlic, drizzle with remaining olive oil and return to oven until golden and cooked through (about 40 minutes longer). Serve hot or at room temperature.

While vegetables are roasting, cut polenta into wedges and lightly dip in a little raw polenta to prevent sticking. Heat oil in a pan and fry wedges until golden on both sides (3-5 minutes).

To serve, divide polenta between 4 plates and top with vegetables. Mix pesto with a little oil to a spoonable consistency and drizzle around the polenta and vegetables.

Spicy Stuffed Eggplants

Glossy purple eggplants are a wonderful substitute for meat when you have vegetarians in the house. Here, the subtle flavour of the flesh benefits from a kick of chilli, the depth of Indian-style spices and the crunch of almonds. The flavour is even better the next day – reheat in a 180°C oven for 10-12 minutes.

Prep time	25 mins
Cook time	1 hour
Serves	4

2 large and
1 medium eggplant

1 tsp ground cumin

1 tsp salt

Spicy Filling
4 tbsp olive oil

2 onions, diced

3 cloves garlic, crushed

1 tsp ground coriander

crushed seeds of
3 cardamom pods

2 tsp ground cumin

½-1 tsp chilli flakes

1 tsp soft brown sugar

1 large red pepper, diced

2 tomatoes, cored and diced

¼ cup coriander leaves

2 kaffir lime leaves, finely chopped, or finely grated zest of 1 lime

2 tbsp lime juice

4 tbsp slivered almonds

Preheat oven to 200°C. Cut the 2 large eggplants in half lengthwise and scoop out the flesh with a sharp spoon or knife to leave a shell about 2cm thick. Brush or spray the insides with a little olive oil. Mix cumin and salt and sprinkle evenly over the inside of the shells. Bake for 30 minutes.

While the eggplant shells are cooking, make the Spicy Filling. Dice the medium eggplant and the reserved flesh of the scooped eggplants. Heat the olive oil in a large pot, add the onions, garlic, ground coriander, cardamom seeds, cumin and chilli and sizzle for 2-3 minutes. Add diced eggplant, sugar, red pepper, tomatoes, coriander leaves and kaffir lime leaves or lime zest. Cover and cook over a medium heat, stirring to prevent sticking, until collapsed (about 15 minutes).

Mix in lime juice, season to taste with salt and pepper and spoon into the baked eggplant shells. Sprinkle 1 tbsp almonds over each eggplant half. Spicy Stuffed Eggplants can be prepared ahead to this point and kept in the fridge for up to 24 hours until needed.

To serve, cook in an oven preheated to 180°C until fragrant and golden (about 30 minutes).

The Ultimate Beef Fillet

An expensive cut like a beef fillet can be worrisome to cook at the last minute, especially if you're busy welcoming people and pouring wine. This restaurant trick takes away the angst. You rare-roast the beef, let it rest, then just prior to serving whack it back into the oven to heat through.

Prep time   10 mins
Cook time   30 mins
Serves   8

1.5kg beef fillet, trimmed

1 tbsp balsamic vinegar

1 tbsp pomegranate molasses

salt and ground black pepper

Cranberry Mint Sauce
½ cup dried cranberries, coarsely chopped

2 tbsp fresh orange juice

1 tbsp pomegranate molasses

¼ cup finely chopped mint

¼ cup toasted pine nuts

1 tbsp boutique extra virgin olive oil

To serve
fresh salad greens

pomegranate seeds (optional)

Preheat oven to 250°C. Place beef on a shallow baking dish lined with baking paper. Rub balsamic vinegar and pomegranate molasses over beef and season to taste with salt and pepper.

When oven is really hot, cook beef for 20 minutes. Remove from oven and allow to rest at room temperature for at least 30 minutes or up to 3 hours.

To make the Cranberry Mint Sauce, stir together dried cranberries, orange juice and pomegranate molasses and leave to stand for 15 minutes or up to 24 hours. Just before serving add mint, pine nuts and olive oil and stir to combine.

When ready to serve, preheat oven to 200°C. Cook beef a further 10 minutes, allow to rest for 5 minutes, then carve into finger-thick slices. Arrange a bed of salad greens on a serving platter, arrange beef slices on top and finish with Cranberry Mint Sauce. Scatter with pomegranate seeds, if using, and serve.

Whether it's a roaring fire, a barbecue or even a candle, the naked flame provides a primal connection with the elements that makes it easy to relax and unwind.

Tuscan Meatballs

These are the lightest, tastiest meatballs of all time. They can be made well ahead of when they are needed, kept chilled and reheated while the pasta cooks.

Prep time	20 mins
Cook time	50-60 mins
Serves	6

500g lean pork mince

3 rashers bacon, finely diced

1 medium onion, grated

2 tbsp chopped parsley

3 tbsp grated parmesan

2 tsp chopped thyme

salt and ground black pepper

200g stale white bread

¼ cup milk

250g ricotta cheese

3 eggs, lightly beaten

Rich Tomato Sauce
2 x 400g cans tomatoes

2 tbsp tomato paste

1 cup red wine

3 cloves garlic, crushed

1 tsp chopped rosemary

1 tsp chopped thyme

1 tbsp sugar

1 cup water

To serve
1 packet dried spaghetti

finely chopped parsley

To prepare the Rich Tomato Sauce, place tomatoes and their juice in a large pot with tomato paste, red wine, garlic, rosemary, thyme, sugar, water and salt and pepper to taste and simmer, uncovered, for 30 minutes, stirring now and then.

While Rich Tomato Sauce is cooking, prepare the meatballs. Preheat oven to 220°C. Place mince and bacon in a large mixing bowl with onion, parsley, parmesan, thyme, 1 tsp salt and pepper to taste. Mix by hand or with a wooden spoon until evenly incorporated.

Whizz bread in a food processor to form crumbs, add milk and pulse to combine. (Or grate the bread into a bowl and stir in the milk). Add to the mince mixture along with ricotta and eggs and mix to combine. The mixture should be light, soft and moist. Using wet hands, form the mixture into balls about the size of golf balls. Place in an oiled baking dish and bake until browned and cooked through (about 20 minutes).

Remove browned meatballs from oven and drain off and discard any fat. Both meatballs and Rich Tomato Sauce can be cooked ahead until this stage, kept in the fridge for up to 48 hours and assembled and reheated when desired.

When ready to serve, pour hot Rich Tomato Sauce over hot meatballs, cover with a lid or tin foil and bake at 180°C for 30 minutes. If you prefer, add the meatballs to the Rich Tomato Sauce and simmer on the stovetop for 20 minutes.

While meatballs are cooking or reheating, cook spaghetti according to packet instructions. Drain and divide between serving bowls. Spoon hot meatballs and sauce over spaghetti and sprinkle with finely chopped parsley to serve.

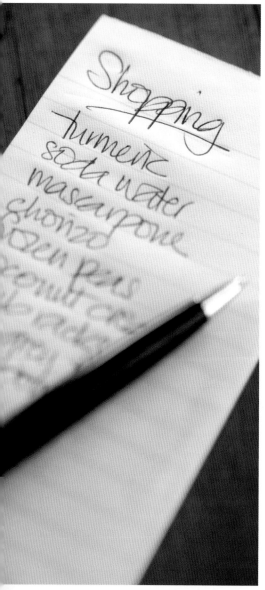

Shopping
turmeric
soda water
mascarpone
chorizo
frozen peas
coconut cream
salads
water

Getting organised

Over the years I have discovered that with a little organisation you can easily whip up meals that make you feel as though you are in your own favourite little neighbourhood restaurant. It's nothing fancy, but the kind of comfortable, tasty, home-cooked food that makes everyone feel relaxed and nurtured – and costs nowhere near as much as it would if you went out to a restaurant.

My strategy is designed around never having to start from scratch. Whenever I can, I make double batches of any recipe that can be frozen – from pies and soups to desserts. That way, inviting friends over for dinner, even at the drop of a hat, becomes easy. A slow-bake or tagine that I had previously cooked in double quantities can be taken out to thaw in the morning, ready to reheat when I get home. The ice cream dessert might also come from the freezer, while some crispy baked crostini from the pantry can be finished with a simple topping. Instead of feeling as though I am facing some kind of culinary marathon, I can relax and enjoy the company of my friends.

By cooking in advance when I have the time and the inclination, I can savour the process of pottering creatively in the kitchen without the pressure of time constraints or a hungry family braying at the door.

During winter weekends I like to cook big pots of soup and freeze them in pottles that I can heat up for an instant meal when I'm home on my own. And I'll often roast a tray of vegetables such as beets, carrots, onions and pumpkin at the start of the week, ready to go into salads, couscous and soups.

I've also found that having a vague eating plan in my head at the beginning of the week really helps to save money and prevent wastage. I use the farmers' market and my garden harvests to roughly map out the week's meals, using whatever is in season as my starting point.

I vary cooking methods from day to day, so our week might include a quick stir-fry, a cook-ahead oven-bake, a pan-fried or soup-style meal, some kind of throw-in-the-oven roast and then a pasta meal served with a salad. That way, our everyday meals feel inventive and interesting but, with a few prep-ahead strategies and a global pantry at my fingertips, they're a cinch to prepare.

Pot-Braised Chicken with Shiitake

This is a great dish because you can throw it in a pot or into the oven and then go and have a shower or a glass of wine to wind down from the day, while it cooks itself to pure succulence. It's equally good served with rice or noodles.

Prep time	10 mins
Cook time	50-90 mins
Serves	4-6

1 whole free-range chicken

½ a lemon

salt and ground black pepper

2 tbsp neutral oil

4cm piece fresh ginger, cut into fine matchsticks

3 tbsp dry sherry

2 tbsp oyster sauce

2 tbsp soy sauce

about ¾ cup water

8-10 shiitake mushrooms, thinly sliced, or 20g dried sliced shiitake soaked in ½ cup water

To serve
finely chopped chives

cooked rice

lightly cooked greens

Pat chicken dry with paper towels and place lemon inside cavity. Season chicken all over with a little salt and lots of pepper. Tie chicken legs together with heatproof string.

Heat oil in a large lidded casserole dish and brown chicken well all over. Remove chicken and drain fat from dish. Return chicken to dish and add ginger, sherry, oyster sauce, soy sauce, water and shiitake or dried shiitake and their soaking liquid.

Bring to a simmer, cover and cook over lowest heat for 50-60 minutes until chicken is fully cooked through, turning after 30 minutes. When turning the chicken, check that the dish has not dried out and add a little more water if necessary. Alternatively, preheat oven to 160°C, place covered casserole dish in the oven and bake for 1½ hours, adding extra water if necessary after 45 minutes.

To check whether the chicken is fully cooked through, insert a skewer into the thickest part of the thigh – if the juices run clear it is done. Pot-Braised Chicken with Shiitake can be prepared ahead to this stage, stored in the fridge for up to 48 hours and reheated when required.

To serve, carve the chicken and serve topped with shiitake pan sauce, garnished with chopped chives and accompanied by cooked rice and lightly cooked greens.

Make-Ahead Lamb Racks

Lamb racks fall into the category of low-effort, high-performance food – there's very little work or skill required to produce an utterly pleasing result. This is a great dinner-party dish because all the preparation is done in advance, ready for a quick flash into the oven. Serve with mashed kumara and wilted greens.

Prep time	15 mins
	+ marinating
Cook time	15 mins
Serves	6-8

3 lamb racks, about 8 bones each, trimmed

2 tbsp fish sauce

2 cloves garlic, crushed

2 tbsp thai sweet chilli sauce

1 tbsp neutral oil

2 tbsp chopped mint leaves

salt and ground black pepper

Chilli Mint Sauce

2 tbsp rice vinegar

1 tbsp sugar

1 tbsp neutral oil

1 tsp fish sauce

finely grated zest and juice of 1 lime

2-3 red chillies, finely chopped

20 mint leaves, chopped

1 spring onion, finely chopped

To serve

mashed golden kumara

wilted watercress or spinach

To make the Chilli Mint Sauce, shake together in a small jar the rice vinegar, sugar, oil, fish sauce, lime zest and juice and chillies. Stand for at least 1 hour or up to 24 hours in the fridge.

To prepare the lamb, combine fish sauce, garlic, chilli sauce, oil and mint and mix through lamb. Marinate for at least 30 minutes or up to 24 hours in the fridge, bringing back to room temperature before cooking.

When you are ready to serve, preheat oven to 240°C. Season lamb with salt and pepper and place in a shallow roasting dish lined with baking paper. Cook for 15 minutes (untrimmed lamb racks with the extra cap of meat and fat still attached will take an extra 4-5 minutes to cook).

Cover and rest for 10 minutes. While lamb is resting, finish the Chilli Mint Sauce by pouring boiling water over the mint leaves, draining at once and refreshing under cold water (this softens their texture and gives them a brilliant green colour). Drain and chop finely. Mix into sauce with spring onion.

Carve lamb racks into sections of 1-2 bones and serve on a bed of mashed kumara and wilted watercress or spinach, with Chilli Mint Sauce drizzled over the top.

Chicken, Fennel and Olive Tagine

Serve this fragrant chicken tagine with israeli couscous tossed with lemon juice, chopped coriander or mint and a handful of chopped nuts such as pistachios.

Prep time   20 mins
Cook time   45-60 mins
Serves   5-6

10-12 skinless chicken thighs, bone in

½ cup flour

salt and ground black pepper

1 tsp paprika

about 5 tbsp olive oil

2 onions, finely diced

4 cloves garlic, finely diced

2 bulbs fennel, finely sliced

400g can cherry tomatoes

3 cups chicken stock

1 strip each lemon and orange peel

¼ cup currants, mixed with 2 tbsp sherry

1 cinnamon quill

2 tsp ground cumin

1 tsp ground ginger

16 threads saffron

1 tsp dried chilli flakes

1-2 green chillies, deseeded and finely chopped

1 tbsp honey

½ cup green olives

If cooking in oven, preheat to 200°C. Place chicken thighs a few pieces at a time in a bag with flour, salt, pepper and paprika. Shake until well coated. Heat 1 tbsp of the olive oil in a large, heavy-based pan and brown chicken in batches, adding more oil as needed. Place chicken in a single layer in a tagine dish, baking dish or pot and set aside.

To make the sauce, heat 2 tbsp olive oil in the pan you have used for browning, add onions and cook over a medium heat, stirring often, until softened but not browned (about 5 minutes). Add garlic and fennel and cook for a further 2 minutes to lightly soften without browning. Add tomatoes, stock, lemon and orange peel, currants in sherry, cinnamon, cumin, ginger, saffron, chilli flakes, fresh chillies and honey. Bring to a simmer and stir well to lift pan brownings. Taste and adjust seasonings.

Pour sauce over chicken. Add olives and bake, covered, in oven for 1 hour or simmer for 45 minutes on stovetop. Remove cinnamon quill and lemon and orange peel before serving.

Chicken, Fennel and Olive Tagine can be stored in the fridge for up to 48 hours or frozen. To serve, bring back to room temperature and then reheat in a 180°C oven until fully heated through (20-30 minutes).

Slow-Baked Pork and Apricots

The tart sweetness of dried apricots beautifully balances the pork in this winter casserole. It's such an easy meal to make in the weekend when you feel like playing in the kitchen, and have ready to pull out of the fridge to reheat for a mid-week dinner. Serve with mashed potato or rice and wilted spinach.

Prep time	20 mins
Cook time	2½ hours
Serves	6

1.5kg shoulder pork, cut into 3-4cm chunks

2 tsp ground cumin

1 tsp smoked paprika

1 tsp salt

ground black pepper

a little olive oil, to brown

2 large onions, cut into thin wedges

1½ tbsp grated fresh ginger

1½ cups chicken stock

finely grated zest and juice of 1 orange

100g dried apricots

1 cup small black olives

¼ cup finely chopped parsley

To serve
wilted spinach

Preheat oven to 150°C. To prepare the pork, mix cumin, paprika, salt and pepper and sprinkle evenly over the pork to lightly coat.

Heat 1 tbsp of the oil in a large, heavy-based pan and brown pork over a high heat, working in batches so as not to overcrowd the pan. Add more oil as needed between batches. Transfer pork to a large ovenproof dish as it browns.

Add onion and ginger to pan and stir over a medium heat until lightly browned (about 5 minutes). Add stock and orange zest and juice and bring to a boil, stirring to lift any pan brownings.

Scatter apricots around the pork and pour the hot sauce over the top. Cover and bake for 2½ hours. Slow-Baked Pork and Apricots can be prepared ahead until this stage, stored in the fridge for up to 48 hours or frozen and reheated when needed. Bring back to room temperature and then reheat in a 180°C oven until fully heated through (20-30 minutes).

When ready to serve, mix olives and parsley into the hot pork. Serve with wilted spinach.

Lamb and White Bean Cassoulet

This heart-warming dish can also be made using other meat such as pork shoulder, rabbit legs or chicken on the bone. It's a good recipe to make a day or two ahead and heat through to serve. Serve with a gutsy red such as a shiraz.

Prep time   15 mins
Cook time   3 hours
Serves   6

6 lamb drums or shanks

salt and ground black pepper

3 cloves garlic, crushed

finely grated zest of 1 lemon

1 cup white wine

2 cups chicken or beef stock

400g can chopped tomatoes

6 pickling onions or shallots, peeled and halved crosswise

2 chorizo sausages, diced in chunks

2 x 400g cans white beans, rinsed and drained

2 bay leaves

2 sprigs fresh thyme

1 tsp chopped rosemary

1 cup shelled and peeled broad beans or soy beans

1 cup fresh or frozen peas

2 tbsp chopped mint leaves

To garnish
finely chopped rosemary leaves

Preheat oven to 220°C. Season lamb liberally with salt and pepper and arrange in a single layer in a large ovenproof dish or roasting dish. Bake until lightly browned (about 45 minutes).

Lift out the lamb and set aside. Drain all fat from the dish and add garlic, lemon zest, white wine, chicken or beef stock, tomatoes, onions or shallots, chorizo, white beans, bay leaves, thyme and rosemary. Stir to combine.

Put lamb back in dish, pressing into liquid so it is semi-submerged. Reduce oven to 160°C, cover dish tightly and cook until tender (about 2¼ hours). Lamb and White Bean Cassoulet can be prepared ahead until this point, cooled and refrigerated for up to 48 hours or frozen until needed, then brought back to room temperature and reheated for 15 minutes on the stovetop, or for 40 minutes in a 180°C oven.

When you are ready to serve, add the beans and peas to the cassoulet in the last 5 minutes of cooking. Adjust seasonings to taste, stir in mint, spoon into large bowls and garnish with extra rosemary to serve.

Coconut Tamarind Prawns

I like to make the Coconut Tamarind Sauce for this curry in bulk and have it on hand in the fridge or freezer. It works really well with vegetables or chicken, but I like it best with prawns. Serve with cooked basmati rice and lime wedges.

Prep time	20 mins
Cook time	20 mins
Serves	6

1.3kg large whole prawns

6 heads bok choy

Coconut Tamarind Sauce

1 large onion, peeled

6 cloves garlic, peeled

4cm piece fresh ginger

1 long red chilli, deseeded

½ cup desiccated coconut

½ cup tamarind concentrate

1 tbsp ground coriander

2 tbsp ground cumin

1 tsp ground turmeric

½ tsp chilli flakes

2 tbsp neutral oil

4 tomatoes, cored and diced

400g can coconut cream

1 cup water

1 whole red or green chilli, slit down the middle (optional)

salt and ground black pepper

To serve
coriander leaves

To make Coconut Tamarind Sauce, roughly chop onion, garlic, ginger and chilli and place in a food processor with coconut, tamarind concentrate, coriander, cumin, turmeric and chilli flakes. Blend to make a smooth paste. Heat oil in a medium-large pot and fry masala paste over medium heat for 5-6 minutes, stirring frequently so it does not catch and burn. Add tomatoes, coconut cream, water and whole chilli, if using, and bring to a boil. Reduce to a simmer and cook for 15 minutes. Season with salt and pepper to taste. Coconut Tamarind Sauce can be prepared ahead and stored in the fridge for up to 48 hours or frozen. Reheat and add prawns and bok choy when needed.

When ready to serve, remove whole chilli. Cut bok choy into 3cm chunks and stir into the boiling curry with the prawns. Cover and simmer until prawns are cooked through and bok choy is wilted but still vibrant green (about 3-4 minutes). Garnish with fresh coriander to serve.

Indonesian Beef Rendang

This rich beef stew simmers away by itself for hours, to emerge meltingly tender. Traditionally it's cooked until almost dry with the coconut oil starting to separate. Once the meat is tender you can decide whether you want it saucier or drier.

Prep time	35 mins
Cook time	3 hours
Serves	6

2 medium red onions, peeled and roughly chopped

6 cloves garlic, peeled

4cm piece fresh ginger, peeled and roughly chopped

1 tsp turmeric

4 red cayenne chillies, deseeded and roughly chopped, or 2 tsp chilli paste

2 kaffir lime leaves, deribbed and shredded, or finely grated zest of 2 limes

400ml coconut cream

1½ cups water

1 tbsp tamarind concentrate (optional)

1.5kg beef shin or cross-cut blade, cut into 4-5cm chunks

1½ tsp salt

2 stalks lemongrass or 1 tbsp finely chopped lemongrass

To serve
poppadoms

Banana Salad (see page 223)

cooked rice

Place red onions, garlic, ginger, turmeric, chillies or chilli paste and kaffir lime leaves or lime zest in a food processor with ¼ cup of the coconut cream and blend to form a smooth curry paste.

Place curry paste in a large pot and sizzle for a couple of minutes. Add the remainder of the coconut cream and the water, tamarind, beef, salt and lemongrass. Bring to a simmer, then cover, reduce heat to lowest possible setting and cook for 2 hours, stirring occasionally. Indonesian Beef Rendang can be prepared in advance to this stage, kept in the fridge for up to 48 hours and brought to room temperature before finishing cooking.

When ready to serve, uncover and cook over a medium heat until the sauce gets really thick and pasty (about 30-40 minutes). At the final stages watch the pot closely and stir often so it does not catch. If the coconut oil starts to separate out and you don't want it to, just add a little more water.

To serve, pile the rendang into a serving dish, removing whole lemongrass stalks, if using. Serve with poppadoms, Banana Salad and cooked rice garnished with black sesame seeds.

It's easy to get stuck in a rut, repeating your failsafe favourite dishes, but nothing beats the thrill of succeeding at something new.

Sides for Spicy Foods

When planning a meal, aim for side dishes that offer a harmony of flavours with your main. These sides are brilliant with spicy dishes such as Indonesian Beef Rendang (see page 220). For other side dishes see pages 160, 184, 280, 287 and 290.

Banana Coconut Salad

Peel and angle-slice 2 firm bananas and toss gently in 2 tbsp lime juice. Mix in ½ cup toasted thread coconut. Serve within an hour or the bananas will start to discolour. Serves 6 as a side dish.

Crisp Cauliflower and Cashew Salad

Place 200g cauliflower florets and 50g roasted, salted cashews in a food processor and pulse a few times to form coarse crumbs. Mix in 2 tbsp finely chopped coriander leaves, 1 tsp grated fresh ginger, 2 tsp neutral oil and a pinch of salt. Serves 6 as a side dish.

Fragrant Basmati Rice

Place 2 cups basmati rice in a pot with 3 cups water, ½ tsp salt, 5 whole cardamom pods, 1 cinnamon stick, ¼ cup thread coconut and the finely grated zest of 1 lime. Stir and bring to a simmer. Cover, reduce to lowest possible heat and cook for 12 minutes. Remove from heat without uncovering and stand for at least 12 minutes or up to 30 minutes. Lift out cardamom pods and cinnamon stick, fluff rice with a fork and serve. Serves 6 as a side dish.

Cucumber and Yoghurt Salad

Deseed and finely dice 3 small lebanese cucumbers, reserving 1 tbsp to use as a garnish. Place the remaining cucumber in a bowl with 1 cup greek yoghurt, ½ tsp ground cumin and 1 tbsp finely chopped mint leaves. Stir to combine. Scoop into a serving dish and garnish with reserved cucumber, a little extra mint and pepper. Serves 6 as a side dish.

Would you like wine with that?

Wine is a fascinating drink – the purest distillation of grape and earth. Someone once remarked that wine is totally democratic – there's one for every palate and every budget. And it's true, just because a wine doesn't carry a high price tag doesn't mean it's not a good wine. On the contrary, such is the glut in wine at the moment that we have never been able to enjoy such good wine for so little money. But there is a lot of jargon, strange nomenclature and elitism around it, which can be very off-putting.

In my book, what to drink when is entirely a matter of personal preference, but if you are looking for a wine to match the food being served, there are a couple of useful guidelines. For example, sweetness in wine reduces the perception of saltiness in food, which is why big, sweet wines like sauternes are often served with salty, ripe cheeses like roquefort, and lighter sweet wines such as riesling or rosé go well with more delicate smoked salmon or ham.

Astringency from tannins (which in excess can cause your mouth to pucker) is what makes wine taste refreshing as it helps clear the palate between mouthfuls. This is why big red wines work so well with rich, deeply flavoured meats. (Young wines have higher tannins, but as they age the tannins fade and the wines become smoother.)

Acid is another important component in wine. It will offset the richness of fat or oiliness in food, which is why high-acid wines such as sauvignon and riesling are often recommended with fish such as salmon. Acid also sharpens our perception of texture and it is very appealing when the textures of the dish and the wine are balanced – for example the smoothness of pinot noir set against a rare-roasted beef fillet, or a gutsier cabernet sauvignon paired with the rougher flavour of a grilled steak.

As a rule of thumb, look to match weight and intensity of flavour – big wines with big dishes, and light, zesty wines with delicate foods. Start with the lightest wines (and foods) at the beginning of your meal and build up from there. Your tastebuds will be dulled if you try to go the other way. Most importantly, have fun experimenting and finding out what tastes good to you.

Ginger Crème Brûlée with Mango

A crunchy caramelised crust gives way to creamy custard and then tropical fruit in this utterly moreish dessert. It's a great party trick to blast the tops with a kitchen blowtorch just before serving, but they work just as well under the grill.

Prep time	20 mins
	+ standing
Cook time	35-45 mins
Serves	6-8

400g can mangos, drained

2 tbsp fresh or bottled passionfruit pulp

6-8 tsp caster sugar

Ginger Custard
1 cup milk

1½ cups cream

⅓ cup sugar

1 tsp vanilla extract

2cm piece ginger, peeled and cut into thin slices

4 eggs, beaten

To serve
fresh mango cheeks

lime slices

a little extra passionfruit pulp

Preheat oven to 140°C. Find an oven dish large enough to hold 6-8 ramekins or cups and fill with water to a depth of 2cm.

To make Ginger Custard, place milk, cream, sugar, vanilla and ginger in a pot over a medium heat. As soon as the mixture comes to a simmer, remove from heat and stand for 10 minutes to allow the ginger flavour to infuse through the milk and cream. Whisk eggs lightly to break up, then stir into the milk and cream mixture. Strain through a fine sieve into a jug.

Purée mangos and mix in passionfruit. Divide between 6-8 ramekins or heatproof cups. Pour the Ginger Custard mixture evenly over the top of the fruit. Place ramekins or cups in the water bath and bake until just set in the centres (about 35-45 minutes). Ginger Crème Brûlée with Mango can be prepared to this stage up to 48 hours ahead and chilled until required.

Before serving, sprinkle the top of each crème brûlée with 1 tsp caster sugar and pop under a hot grill, watching carefully, until golden brown and lightly caramelised (or place on a heatproof bench or tray and use a blowtorch to caramelise the tops). Serve immediately or return to fridge for up to an hour. Serve with a garnish of fresh mango, lime and passionfruit.

Pistachio Praline Semifreddo

You can make this luscious ice cream dessert well ahead of time as it will keep for 2-3 weeks in a sealed container in the freezer.

Prep time	30 mins
	+ cooling
	+ freezing
Serves	8

Semifreddo Base

5 egg whites

½ cup runny honey

1 cup cream

1 tsp vanilla extract

Pistachio Praline

½ cup sugar

¼ cup honey

1 cup shelled, unsalted pistachios

To make the Semifreddo Base, line a sponge roll tin or shallow container with baking paper. Place the egg whites in a clean mixing bowl and beat to soft peaks. Gradually add the runny honey, beating until mixture is thick and glossy. In a separate bowl, whisk the cream and vanilla to soft peaks. Gently fold the two mixtures together (do not beat or the egg whites will collapse). Transfer to sponge roll tin or shallow container and freeze while you prepare the praline.

To make the Pistachio Praline, line a metal tray with baking paper. Place sugar in a clean pot with honey and heat gently until sugar has dissolved. Swirl the pot occasionally but do not stir. To prevent mixture from crystallising, wet a pastry brush with water and run this around the inside of the pot. When mixture turns a rich golden caramel (about 15 minutes) remove it from the heat, add the pistachios, swirl to coat and tip onto prepared tray, tilting tray to spread in a thin layer. Allow to cool and harden. Set aside half the Pistachio Praline to use as a garnish. Place the other half in a paper bag and crush into coarse crumbs with a rolling pin.

After the Semifreddo Base has been in the freezer for 2 hours, remove and stir through the crumbled Pistachio Praline. Return to the freezer for at least another 2 hours before serving.

To serve, use a round cutter to cut semifreddo into portions. Garnish with large chunks of reserved Pistachio Praline.

Feeling comfortable in someone else's home and enjoying food they have prepared is one of life's great pleasures.

Caramel Bread Puddings

Here I've brought the classic bread and butter pudding upmarket and up to date by adding apples and dried cranberries. I think it looks more special baked in individual ramekins or cups but you could make it in one big dish if you prefer. Serve with vanilla ice cream or pouring cream on the side.

Prep time	20 mins
	+ standing
Cook time	35-50 mins
Serves	6

7 slices toast bread
or 3 croissants

butter, for greasing

2 cooking apples, peeled, cored and thinly sliced

⅓ cup dried cranberries or currants

Caramel Custard

½ cup sugar

2 tbsp water

3 cups milk

4 eggs

½ tsp ground nutmeg or cardamom

2 tsp vanilla extract

To make Caramel Custard, heat sugar and water in a medium pot, stirring until sugar has dissolved. Boil mixture without stirring until it forms a deep, rich caramel (about 5 minutes). Remove from heat and slowly add 1 cup of the milk, stirring until caramel is dissolved. Add remaining milk. Whisk in the eggs, nutmeg and vanilla.

Remove crusts from bread and cut each slice into 4 triangles, or angle-slice each croissant into 4-5 slices. Grease 6 ramekins or heatproof cups or a shallow 30cm baking dish with a little butter. Interleave bread or croissant slices with apple slices in prepared ramekins, cups or baking dish. Sprinkle with dried cranberries or currants and pour the Caramel Custard over the top. Stand for at least 30 minutes or chill for up to 24 hours and bring back to room temperature before cooking.

When ready to serve, preheat oven to 160°C. Bake the bread puddings until puffed and golden (about 50 minutes for a single dish or 35-40 minutes for ramekins or cups). Serve hot or at room temperature.

Baked Ricotta and Apricot Cheesecakes

Dense and tangy, these baked Italian desserts make a special treat that can be prepared well ahead of time. The mixture can also be cooked as one big cheesecake – use a 26cm tin and bake for 1 hour. Unlike many cheesecakes, which ooze calories, this recipe uses low-fat ricotta instead of cream or cream cheese.

Prep time	15 mins
Cook time	25-35 mins
Serves	6-8

1 tbsp butter, for greasing

2 tbsp sugar

½ cup caster sugar

6 egg yolks

500g low-fat ricotta

finely grated zest of 2 oranges

¼ cup orange juice

1 tsp vanilla extract

½ tsp almond essence

1 cup dried apricots, finely diced

½ cup self-raising flour

¼ cup slivered almonds

To dust
icing sugar

Preheat oven to 180°C. Grease 6-8 ramekins or heatproof cups with butter. Spoon in sugar and shake to coat base and sides, discarding any excess.

In a mixing bowl or electric mixer beat caster sugar and egg yolks together until thick and creamy. Fold through ricotta, orange zest, orange juice, vanilla extract and almond essence. Mix apricots through the flour (this stops them sinking into the mixture), then fold the flour and apricots into the ricotta mixture.

Divide mixture between prepared ramekins or cups and scatter slivered almonds on top. Bake for 25-35 minutes or until the tops bounce back when pressed and a skewer inserted in the centre comes out clean.

Allow cheesecakes to cool for 10 minutes before removing from the oven. Cover and chill for at least 2 hours before serving. They will keep for up to 24 hours in the fridge. Dust with icing sugar to serve.

New York Cheesecake

This crustless New York-style cheesecake is dreamily creamy. It's a handy recipe to include when you're planning the menu for a special dinner because it's best made in advance and chilled until serving. It's sensationally rich so serve it in small portions. Any leftovers will keep happily in the fridge.

Prep time	10 mins
Cook time	75 mins
	+ sitting
Serves	10-12

butter, for greasing

500g cream cheese

500g sour cream

1 cup sugar

3 eggs

2 tsp vanilla extract

finely grated zest of ½ a lemon

2 tbsp lemon juice

Passionfruit Topping
flesh of 6 passionfruit

2 tbsp sugar

1 tsp cornflour

To serve (optional)
fresh blueberries

Preheat oven to 150°C. Line a 23cm springform cake tin with baking paper and grease the sides with a little butter.

Place cream cheese, sour cream, sugar, eggs, vanilla and lemon zest and juice in a food processor or electric mixer and whizz or mix until smooth (about 1 minute).

Pour mixture into prepared tin, bake for 1¼ hours, then turn off the oven and leave the cheesecake in the oven with the door open for 1 hour. Chill the cheesecake for at least 4 hours before removing it from the tin. It will keep for 4-5 days in a covered container in the fridge.

To make the Passionfruit Topping, mix passionfruit, sugar and cornflour together and heat until simmering and very lightly thickened. Cool and refrigerate if not using at once.

Just before serving, spoon the Passionfruit Topping over the cheesecake. Serve garnished with fresh blueberries, if using.

It's easy to tweak recipes to make the most of whatever fresh seasonal ingredients are at hand. In this way you can explore your own creativity.

Ginger Steamed Pudding

I'm sure people made steamed puddings in the old days because they were a cheap way to fill everyone up and leave them with smiles on their faces. It's a strategy that still works – especially on a cold winter night. This pudding can be made ahead and reheated in the microwave for 2-3 minutes or re-steamed for 20-30 minutes.

Prep time   15 mins
Cook time   1½ hours
Serves   6-8

120g butter,
plus extra for greasing

1 packed cup brown sugar

2 eggs

5 tbsp golden syrup

1¼ cups self-raising flour

½ tsp baking soda

2 tsp ground ginger

2 tsp mixed spice

finely grated zest of ½ lemon

½ cup roughly chopped
crystallised ginger

To serve
whipped cream, custard
or ice cream

In a mixing bowl or electric mixer, beat butter and sugar until pale and creamy. Beat in eggs and 1 tbsp of the golden syrup. Fold in flour, baking soda, ground ginger, mixed spice, lemon zest and 2 tbsp of the crystallised ginger.

Grease a 2-litre pudding bowl or metal basin with butter. Spoon the remaining 4 tbsp golden syrup into the bottom of the pudding bowl and sprinkle in the rest of the crystallised ginger. Spoon in the pudding mixture and smooth the top. Place pudding bowl on a clean teatowel, draw up sides to enclose the bowl and secure with a clothes peg or twist tie.

Place a small saucer or trivet in the bottom of a large pot and place the wrapped pudding on top (this stops the pudding from touching the base of the pot and overcooking). Fill the pot with enough water to come a third of the way up the outside of the pudding bowl. Cover pot tightly, place on stovetop and bring water to a simmer. Steam pudding 1½ hours. Check occasionally and replenish water if it gets too low – don't let it dry out.

Remove pot from heat and allow to stand for 5 minutes before lifting out the wrapped pudding and untying the cloth cover. Turn pudding out onto a serving plate. Serve hot, cut into wedges with whipped cream, custard or ice cream.

Italian-Inspired
Dinner for Friends

I like to plan my menus within the frame of a single culinary culture. Most of the preparation for this Italian-themed meal can be done in advance. Salute!

A bowl of marinated olives

White Bean and Rocket Bruschetta, page 244

∾

Tuscan Meatballs, page 202

Spaghetti

Radicchio Salad with Blue Cheese, page 280

∾

Baked Ricotta and
Apricot Cheesecakes, page 232

∾

A bottle of merlot

A Vegetarian Feast

Serving only meat-free meals when vegetarian friends visit makes them feel so welcome. This satisfying menu will convert even the most hard-core carnivore.

A bowl of spicy roasted chickpeas

∽

Cauliflower Broccoli Fritters
with Mango Dip, page 256

∽

Spicy Stuffed Eggplants, page 196

Spiced Roast Potatoes, page 290

∽

Ginger Crème Brûlée with Mango, page 226

∽

A bottle of pinot noir

For prep plans, shopping lists and more menus
see annabel-langbein.com

party plates

A platter of little nibbles gets the party started.

I find it much more relaxing to invite people over for a drink than to meet them at a bar or restaurant where the food is often disappointing and expensive. I love being able to wing impromptu gatherings for a few friends, inviting them to pop in to celebrate a win or a special occasion – or just to toast the end of the week.

The great thing about inviting people on the spur of the moment is that they don't have any huge culinary expectations. I like to serve a bowl of punch or a zingy cocktail to start things rolling, then I put out a decent wedge of cheese and some olives and serve a dip with bread and crackers. If extra people arrive, I grill more bread and slather it with pesto and feta, or chop up raw vegetable crudités to serve with a bowl of olive oil and balsamic vinegar or dukkah.

Even when I do have the luxury of time to prepare in advance, I try to avoid the temptation to make food that is too complicated. I love stand-up parties at which tasty little nibbles are passed around, but I serve no more than four or six different types of finger food, allowing two or three pieces of each for each person and aiming for a collection of dishes that feels harmonious and satisfying. There is nothing worse than feeling as though your insides resemble the fridges of 20 different caterers.

Once you have figured out what you are going to eat and drink, the actual preparation is easy – so much can be organised ahead of time. Just make sure you leave yourself half an hour to escape from the kitchen before everyone arrives, or you'll be sick of the sight of food before the evening has even started. And if everyone is having a good time it's nice to be able to say "stay for dinner" – never a drama if you've got some soup or a casserole in the freezer, or the ingredients for a quick pasta in your pantry.

Bruschetta Toppings

To make bruschetta, cut slices from a county loaf, brush with olive oil and grill or bake at about 160°C until crisp. To make crostini, use thinner rounds of french bread. If not using at once, store bruschetta or crostini in an airtight container and refresh in a 180°C oven for 5 minutes before using.

Grated Zucchini and Feta Bruschetta

To make Grated Zucchini and Feta, coarsely grate 3 zucchini onto a clean teatowel, pull up the sides, twist and squeeze tightly to remove liquid. Heat 3 tbsp olive oil in a large frypan and add zucchini, 2 crushed cloves garlic, a pinch of chilli flakes and the finely grated zest of 1 lemon. Stir-fry over medium heat until zucchini has softened without browning (about 5 minutes). Remove from heat and cool 5 minutes. Mix in 50g crumbled feta and 10-12 finely torn basil leaves and season to taste. To serve, spoon onto about 16 bruschetta or 24 crostini bases. Serves 4-6 as a snack or appetiser. Grated Zucchini and Feta also makes a lovely side dish with meat or fish.

Bruschetta with Green Goddess Topping

To make Green Goddess Topping, mash the flesh of two just-ripe avocados with 3 tbsp Parsley Pesto (see page 254). Season to taste. To serve, spread generously onto about 16 bruschetta or 24 crostini bases and drizzle with lemon juice. Serves 4-6 as a snack or appetiser.

White Bean and Rocket Bruschetta

To make White Bean Purée, rinse and drain a 400g can white beans. Place in a pot with 2 cloves crushed garlic, 4 tbsp olive oil, the finely grated zest of 1 lemon and a pinch of chilli flakes. Cook over a low heat for 5 minutes, then add 1 tbsp lemon juice. Mash to a rough purée, thinning with a little water if required, and season to taste. Add a generous handful of finely chopped rocket or spinach and stir over heat for a minute to wilt. Cool. To serve, spoon onto about 16 bruschetta or 24 crostini bases and drizzle with boutique extra virgin olive oil. Serves 4-6 as a snack or appetiser. White Bean Purée is also fantastic served as a hot side dish with chicken or lamb.

Mini Chicken Tortilla Cups

Press flour tortillas into mini-muffin pans and bake until crisp to make these crunchy little mouthfuls. You can also use egg wonton wrappers. For a more substantial dish, the chicken, olive and egg filling mixture is delicious encased between savoury shortcrust pastry or empanada dough to make little pies.

Prep time	30 mins
Cook time	30 mins
Makes	48 mini cups

12 medium (20cm diameter) flour tortillas

2 tbsp neutral oil

400g chicken mince

1 stalk celery, finely diced

1 onion, finely diced

1 tsp crushed garlic

2 tbsp tomato paste

1 tsp chilli powder

1 tsp mixed herbs

2 tsp ground cumin

1 tsp soft brown sugar

½ cup white wine or water

1 tsp salt

1 tsp ground black pepper

½ cup stoned olives, chopped

2 hard-boiled eggs, chopped

To garnish
coriander leaves

Preheat oven to 170°C. Use an 8cm cookie cutter to cut circles from the tortillas. Press into mini-muffin pans and lightly spray with oil. Bake until crisp (about 12-15 minutes). If not using at once, store in an airtight container and refresh in a 180°C oven for 5 minutes before using.

Heat oil in a heavy-based frypan, add chicken mince and cook over high heat until brown (about 5 minutes). Remove from pan and set aside. Add celery, onion, garlic and tomato paste to pan and cook over medium heat until onion is soft (about 5 minutes). Return chicken to pan and add chilli, mixed herbs, cumin, sugar, wine or water, salt and pepper. Simmer over low heat, stirring often, for about 15 minutes. The mixture should be quite dry.

Remove from heat and mix in olives and eggs. Place 1 heaped tsp mixture into each tortilla cup and garnish with coriander leaves. Serve warm or at room temperature.

Smoked Fish Morsels

These retro-style vol-au-vents are a timelessly popular party snack that I have brought up to date by using crème fraiche instead of white sauce. Cook the pastry cases and prepare the filling in advance, then put them together at the last minute and warm them through. Make large vol-au-vents for an easy, delicious lunch.

Prep time	20 mins
Cook time	16-18 mins
Makes	16

2 sheets flaky puff pastry

1 lightly beaten egg, to glaze

Smoked Fish Cream
150g smoked fish, flaked

¼ cup crème fraiche

2 tbsp lemon juice

1 tbsp finely chopped parsley

a pinch of freshly grated nutmeg

Preheat oven to 200°C and line a baking tray with baking paper. Use a 6cm cookie cutter to cut 16 circles from each sheet of pastry. Place half the circles on the baking paper and brush with egg glaze.

Using a 4cm cookie cutter or a sharp knife, cut a smaller circle in the centre of the remaining 16 circles and lift out the centres to make doughnut shapes. Stack 1 doughnut shape on top of each whole circle on the baking paper and brush with egg glaze.

Bake until the pastry has puffed up and is golden brown (about 10 minutes). Allow to cool. The vol-au-vent cases can be made several days in advance and stored in an airtight container until needed.

To make Smoked Fish Cream, stir together smoked fish, crème fraiche, lemon juice, parsley and nutmeg. Smoked Fish Cream can be made up to a day in advance and chilled until needed.

Up to 30 minutes before serving, spoon Smoked Fish Cream into vol-au-vent pastry cases. When ready to serve, preheat oven to 180°C and bake until warmed through (about 6-8 minutes).

Light-as-Air Savoury Tarts

With a packet of frozen puff pastry sheets in the freezer you can whip up piping hot savoury tarts in a flash. They can be prepped ready to cook in advance, kept on trays in the fridge and baked until golden in a hot oven at the last minute.

Broccoli, Blue Cheese and Almond Tarts

Very finely chop 100g broccoli florets and mix with 1 tbsp olive oil, 60g blue cheese and 2 tbsp chopped raw almonds. Cut 1 sheet flaky puff pastry into 8 rectangles (2 rows x 4 rows). Arrange on a baking tray lined with baking paper. Divide broccoli mixture between pastry rectangles and bake at 200°C until puffed and golden (about 10-12 minutes). Makes 8.

Anchovy Twists

Cut 1 sheet of flaky puff pastry into 18 rectangles (3 rows x 6 rows). Drain oil from 9 canned anchovies and halve them lengthwise. Place half an anchovy diagonally across each pastry rectangle, twist pastry 2 or 3 times to form a loose spiral and place on a baking tray lined with baking paper. Bake at 200°C until puffed and golden (about 10-12 minutes). These can be made ahead of time, stored in an airtight container and refreshed in a hot oven for 3 to 4 minutes before serving. Makes 18.

Asparagus Tarts

Cut 1 sheet of flaky puff pastry into 8 rectangles (2 rows x 4 rows). Arrange on a baking tray lined with baking paper. Trim 8 spears of asparagus, cut in half and place 2 halves on each pastry rectangle. Top liberally with grated pecorino or parmesan (about 50g total), scatter with finely grated lemon zest, season to taste and drizzle with a few drops of olive oil. Bake at 200°C until puffed and golden (about 10-12 minutes). Makes 8.

Tomato, Pesto and Feta Tartlets

Use a 7cm cookie cutter to cut 9 circles from a sheet of flaky puff pastry. Arrange on a baking tray lined with baking paper and top each with ½ tsp pesto, 2-3 thin slices tomato and crumbled feta (50g total). Bake at 200°C until puffed and golden (about 10-12 minutes). Makes 9.

Gather a bunch of
fun-loving people,
add wine, good
food and sparkling
conversation and
you have the recipe
for a great night.

Quick Platter Ideas

You don't have to be a whizz-bang cook to be a fabulous host. These quick platter combinations call for the freshest ingredients presented simply but beautifully.

Crudité with Curry Mayo and Balsamic Oil Dips

Trim raw vegetables of your choice and slice into thin strips. Purple and orange carrots, radicchio leaves, asparagus spears, lebanese cucumbers, beans, cauliflower florets, red peppers and radishes all work well. To make Curry Mayo, whisk ½ cup good-quality mayonnaise with 3 tsp lime or lemon juice, 1 tsp good-quality curry powder and ½ tsp soft brown sugar. To make Balsamic Oil, pour 2 tbsp balsamic vinegar into a small serving dish with 4 tbsp boutique extra virgin olive oil, salt and pepper. Arrange vegetables and dips on a platter. Serves 6-8.

Cheese with Prosciutto and Bread

When putting together a cheese platter, I prefer to use just one or two fabulous cheeses instead of lots of small segments of random cheeses. Buy a large slice of your favourite cheese – I usually go for pecorino, a lovely blue or a creamy chèvre – and store it in the fridge wrapped in waxed paper. About an hour before serving allow it to come to room temperature. Serve with thinly sliced prosciutto, a crusty cob loaf and a glass of pinot noir.

Asparagus Spears with Parsley Pesto

To make Parsley Pesto, purée a large bunch each of parsley and mint leaves, 2 roughly chopped cloves garlic, ¼ cup grated parmesan, ¼ cup toasted almonds, salt and pepper. When smooth add ½ cup olive oil, adjusting quantity if necessary to reach dipping consistency. Drop about 24 trimmed asparagus spears into a pot of boiling salted water, boil 3 minutes then drain and refresh under cold water. Drain and place on a platter with a dish of Parsley Pesto. Any unused pesto can be stored in the fridge for 2 weeks or frozen for later use. Serves 6-8.

Smoked Salmon au Naturel

Serve a piece of hot-smoked salmon with caperberries, sliced turkish bread or ciabatta and a simple sauce made by mixing 1 cup light sour cream, 2 tbsp horseradish sauce, 1 tbsp lemon juice, salt and pepper. Accompany with lemon wedges. Serves 6-8.

Cauliflower Broccoli Fritters with Mango Dip

Here's an easy way to make something out of nothing. A few spices transform cauliflower and broccoli into tender fritters, which can be cooked ahead of time and reheated in a hot oven for 4-5 minutes before serving with a fruity, tangy dip.

Prep time   15 mins
Cook time   15 mins
Makes   18 fritters

½ cup flour or rice flour

¼ tsp baking soda

1 tsp curry powder

1 tsp turmeric

½ tsp chopped fennel seeds

1 tsp grated fresh ginger

2 eggs

¼ cup milk or water

½ tsp salt

½ tsp ground black pepper

300g cauliflower or broccoli
or a mixture of both

1 spring onion, finely sliced

2 tbsp chopped coriander

a little neutral oil, for frying

Mango Dip
1 mango or ½ can mangos

2 tbsp lime juice

2 tbsp chopped coriander

½ cup mango chutney

To garnish
sprigs of fresh coriander

To make Mango Dip, peel the mango and cut the flesh off the stone, or if using canned mangos drain off the juice and discard. Purée the mango flesh with lime juice, coriander and mango chutney. Store in the fridge for up to 24 hours until needed.

To make fritters, mix flour with soda, curry powder, turmeric, fennel seeds, ginger, eggs, milk or water and salt and pepper to form a smooth, thick batter. Cut cauliflower and/or broccoli into chunks and pulse to a fine couscous-like crumb in a food processor (or finely chop to a crumb). Mix into batter with spring onion and coriander and stir to evenly combine.

Heat 2 tbsp oil in a heavy-based frypan and add small spoonfuls of mixture. Fry in batches over medium heat until golden and cooked through (about 2 minutes each side), flipping as bubbles form. Add a little more oil to the pan between batches as needed. Transfer cooked fritters to a plate lined with paper towels to absorb excess oil.

Serve fritters hot or warm, garnished with coriander and accompanied by Mango Dip.

Oysters on Brown Bread

The best oysters come from the coldest water – they have a sweet flavour and meaty, almost crisp, texture. When they are really fresh you just want to taste their briny essence without too much embellishment. I prefer mine with a hint of lemon and wine vinegar, but you could use wasabi, capers or herbs instead.

| Prep time | 5 mins |
| Serves | 4-6 as an appetiser |

about 3 tbsp butter, at room temperature

a little finely grated lemon zest or soft herbs

3 slices dense wholegrain bread

12 chilled oysters

2 tsp chardonnay vinegar or champagne vinegar or lemon juice

ground black pepper

Place butter in a bowl with lemon zest or herbs and mix to combine. Spread bread slices with the lemon or herb butter and then trim off the crusts. Cut each slice into 4 squares. The bread can be prepared in advance to this stage and covered with a moist paper towel until needed.

Just before serving, drain brine from oysters and discard. Add vinegar or lemon juice to oysters and stir gently to coat. Place an oyster on top of each piece of bread, season with a little freshly ground black pepper and serve at once.

Oysters with Kilpatrick Topping

Here's my take on the classic Oysters Kilpatrick. It's perfect for whetting appetites before dinner, or as a platter to hand around at a cocktail party. I get the oysters ready before everyone arrives, keep them in the fridge and blast them under the grill just before serving.

Prep time	5 mins
Cook time	2-3 mins
Serves	6-8 as an appetiser

4 rashers streaky bacon, very finely diced

neutral oil, for frying

24 oysters on the half-shell

2 tbsp worcestershire sauce

4 tbsp melted butter

2 tsp lemon juice

1 tsp finely chopped parsley leaves

salt and ground black pepper

Fry bacon in a little oil until very crispy. Drain and discard fat. Place the oysters in their shells in a shallow baking dish or tray and scatter bacon over the top.

Mix together worcestershire sauce, melted butter, lemon juice, parsley and salt and pepper to taste. Spoon about ½ tsp of mixture over each oyster. The oysters can be prepared ahead until this point and stored covered in the fridge for up to 4 hours until needed.

When ready to serve, place the tray of oysters under a preheated grill for 2-3 minutes until they are just warmed through. Serve immediately.

Mussels Florentine

New Zealand's green-lipped mussels are unsurpassed anywhere in the world. This is one of my favourite ways of eating them, nestled on a bed of creamy spinach with a crumbling of sweet, nutty gruyère cheese on top.

Prep time	15 mins
Cook time	8-10 mins
Serves	6 as an appetiser

18 cleaned mussels in their shells

1 tbsp butter

2 cloves garlic, crushed

⅓ cup cream

5 handfuls (125g) baby spinach leaves or destemmed regular spinach, chopped

1 tbsp chopped dill or fennel or parsley

a pinch of freshly grated nutmeg

salt and ground black pepper

2-3 tbsp coarsely grated gruyère cheese

Place mussels in a pot with a splash of water. Cover tightly and cook over a high heat until opened (3-5 minutes). Drain, discarding the cooking liquid and any mussels that have not opened. Take mussels out of shells, removing any remaining beards and arranging half the shells in a shallow oven dish lined with baking paper. Discard the remaining shells.

Heat butter in the same pot the mussels were cooked in, add garlic and allow to sizzle for about 1 minute without browning. Add cream, spinach and dill or fennel or parsley and toss over heat until spinach is wilted. Remove from the heat and season with nutmeg and salt and pepper to taste.

Divide spinach mixture between the 18 half shells, using about 2 tsp in each shell. Toss the mussels briefly in the cream mixture left in the pot and then return a single mussel to each shell on top of spinach. Mussels Florentine can be prepared ahead to this point and chilled until needed.

When ready to serve, sprinkle a little gruyère on top of the mussels and place under a hot grill for 3-4 minutes until bubbling and golden. Transfer to a platter and serve at once.

If you're relaxed everyone else will be too. Keep the food simple so you're not stressing in the kitchen.

celebrations

Sometimes you want to pull out all the stops.

In my early twenties I backpacked around South America, spending almost two years on the road, eking out my hard-earned savings with two-dollar meals, grotty hotel rooms and hitched rides. It was the most fantastic adventure of my life. But as the days counted down towards my first Christmas, I felt the twang of homesickness.

I yearned to be with my family, eat turkey and pavlova, exchange presents and loll about in that state of excess that, in our house anyway, defined Christmas Day.

Eventually I was invited to join a friend for his family Christmas in the north of Colombia. My spirits lifted as I thought I would finally get my Christmas fix. But it was not to be. Alberto's mother was not impressed by being asked to share her Christmas with some blonde gringo foreigner and wherever I happened to be in the house she would come in, muttering, and turn off the light. Welcome – not.

On Christmas morning, Alberto's father decided that as a special guest I should be treated to a Colombian delicacy. We drove to the abattoir, where they bought a bucket of blood. They brought it home, boiled it in a huge pot, then scoffed it with relish. All these years later the thought still makes my bile rise. They were so happy, celebrating Christmas as they always had – no gargantuan feast, no turkey, no cake, no presents. I was miserable, desperate for the cocooning bosom of my family and my culture.

It made me realise how important the traditions, rituals and celebrations of our families and cultures are, and how they anchor our lives. Around the table we share food and ideas, laugh and debate, bind families together and cement friendships. When we are young, traditions can seem outdated and boring, even claustrophobic and irrelevant, but as we grow older we cherish the seasonal celebrations in which we find a sense of belonging.

Crab Shooters

These Crab Shooters are like a Bloody Mary with a hint of the ocean. I have childhood memories of a non-alcoholic version being served up as a party starter, using canned shrimps. In fact, they taste good with all kinds of seafood, but I particularly love them with the sweetness of crab meat.

| Prep time | 5 mins |
| Serves | 8-12 as an appetiser |

350g cooked fresh crab meat or 2 x 170g cans crab meat, drained

Bloody Mary Mix
1 litre chilled tomato juice

2 tbsp worcestershire sauce

2 tbsp lemon juice

2 tsp tabasco sauce

2 tbsp very finely chopped celery (optional)

¼-½ cup vodka (optional)

salt and ground black pepper

To serve
juice of 1 lime or lemon

To make Bloody Mary Mix, stir tomato juice in a jug with worcestershire sauce, lemon juice and tabasco, and celery and vodka, if using. Season to taste with salt and pepper. Bloody Mary Mix can be prepared in advance and kept in the fridge for up to 48 hours until required.

When ready to serve, stir half the crab meat into the Bloody Mary Mix. Divide between 8-12 shot glasses, top with reserved crab meat and finish with a squeeze of lime or lemon juice.

Melon Platter with Mint and Prosciutto

Sometimes you don't really need a recipe. This idea for a serve-yourself salad plate uses the classic combination of melon and prosciutto as a starting point. I've added watercress, mint and pistachios, but you could use folds of smoked salmon instead of prosciutto or macadamias instead of pistachios.

Prep time   15 mins
Serves   8-10
               as a starter

250-300g fresh watercress tips or rocket leaves

½ rock melon, deseeded, peeled and thinly sliced

½ honeydew melon, deseeded, peeled and thinly sliced

2 tbsp lime juice

20 mint leaves, finely torn

2 limes, halved and very thinly sliced

10-12 very thin slices prosciutto

1 cup toasted pistachios (optional)

To garnish
a sprig of mint

Arrange watercress tips or rocket leaves on a large platter and top with slices of rock melon and honeydew melon.

Drizzle with lime juice and scatter with mint leaves and lime slices. Roll prosciutto slices into loose rosette shapes and arrange over the platter. Sprinkle with pistachios, if using. Garnish with a sprig of mint and serve.

Melon Platter with Mint and Prosciutto can be assembled up to an hour before serving and kept in the fridge until needed.

Natalie

Setting the scene

I'm a dress-for-dinner kind of gal. It's something my mother did every night when we were growing up, which created a lovely sense of ritual around dinnertime. I like the change in gear it brings to the end of the day, as if you're going out for dinner without having to go anywhere.

My mother always laid a beautiful table, lit candles and filled a big jug with water, even if we were just having a really simple family dinner by ourselves. The idea of setting the scene – spreading a tablecloth, putting flowers or a bowl of fruit on the table – all adds up to creating a sense of care and ritual and occasion.

On a welcoming table, even the simplest food feels special. The stage is set, upon which you can relax, share a conversation and take some time out. In such a simple way you can make your evening meals a little high point in the day, a breather from the rush and bustle of city life and a chance to reconnect with people you care about.

And every now and then, a special event comes along that makes you want to really go to town. Maybe it's a special-occasion dinner, a birthday celebration with the extended family, or every foodie's favourite day of the year, Christmas. This is the time to haul out your grandma's old china dinner set, polish the silverware and iron your favourite linen napkins – but that doesn't mean your food needs to be complicated or showy.

Because the antipodean Christmas falls in summer, we're liberated from traditions built up in another climate on the other side of the world. We drag a table out into the garden, open a brightly coloured sun umbrella and choose elements from our own natural world to adorn our dinner setting. Just the simple fact of stepping out of a formal dining setting helps everyone – including you – to relax.

Just before people arrive, I'll put on some music and pop a tray of spiced almonds or a loaf of bread in the oven to warm up and fill the house with welcoming aromas.

Feeling relaxed and cosy at home is one of life's great pleasures. Soft lighting, cruisy music, simple, good food, a sense of warmth, conviviality and comfort… you'll never want to leave the table.

Even the simplest food looks sensational
when it's served on a table laid with style.
The mood is set for a celebration.

Sake and Ginger Roasted Salmon

This is such a useful special-occasion dish because you marinate the salmon and make the Pickled Cucumber in advance and leave it in the fridge until you're ready to eat. Then the salmon takes only about 10 minutes to cook to that melting state of medium-rareness.

Prep time — 15 mins
+ marinating
Cook time — 10 mins
Serves — 6-8

½ cup sake

2 tbsp grated fresh ginger

1 tbsp honey

½ cup soy sauce or tamari

1 side salmon (about 500g), skin on, deboned

Pickled Cucumber
5 lebanese cucumbers

6 tbsp boiling water

2 tsp sugar

2 tbsp white wine vinegar

1 tsp salt

½ tsp fine white pepper

1 red chilli, deseeded and chopped

2 tsp sesame oil

70g pickled ginger, finely chopped

To serve
2 tbsp black sesame seeds

Mix sake with ginger, honey and soy sauce or tamari in a shallow tray. Place salmon skin side up in the marinade, cover and chill for at least 8 hours or up to 24 hours. Remove from fridge 30 minutes before cooking to return to room temperature.

While the salmon is marinating, make the Picked Cucumber. Halve the cucumbers lengthwise, scoop out and discard the seeds and angle-slice the flesh. Place in a bowl. Mix together the boiling water, sugar, vinegar, salt, white pepper, chilli, sesame oil and pickled ginger and pour over the cucumbers. Marinate for at least 30 minutes or up to 24 hours in the fridge. Drain before serving.

When ready to cook, preheat oven to 250°C. Lift salmon out of marinade, discard marinade and place salmon skin side down on a shallow baking dish lined with baking paper. Roast for 10 minutes – it should be very rare. Remove from oven, cover and leave on the bench to cool for at least 30 minutes.

To serve, transfer the salmon to a serving dish, scatter Pickled Cucumber over the top and sprinkle with black sesame seeds.

Crisp and Crunchy Salads

Because these tasty salads travel well they're useful to take as a contribution to a shared meal or barbecue or to work in your lunchbox. For other useful portable salads see page 184. For other side dishes see pages 223 and 287.

Asian Slaw with Sake Dressing

Place 2 cups finely shredded chinese cabbage or regular cabbage in a large bowl. Work between your fingers to soften and moisten. Add 1 cup bean sprouts, 2 tbsp chopped coriander, 1 tbsp chopped chives, ¼ cup chopped toasted peanuts and 2 tbsp sesame seeds and toss to evenly combine. To make Sake Dressing, shake 1 tsp sesame oil, 1 tsp soy sauce, 2 tsp sake or dry sherry and 2 tsp rice vinegar in a small jar. Just before serving, toss Sake Dressing through Asian Slaw. Serves 4 as a side dish to curries or Asian meals.

Radicchio Salad with Blue Cheese

Finely slice 1 head of radicchio, roughly chop 2 heads of witloof and place in a bowl. Fry 100g very finely diced bacon in 2 tbsp olive oil until very crispy. Remove from heat and add 1 tbsp red wine vinegar or sherry vinegar and ½ tsp dijon mustard. Stir to incorporate and season to taste with salt, pepper and a pinch of sugar. Allow to cool, then toss through radicchio and witloof. Scatter 100g crumbled blue cheese over the top and toss gently to combine. Serves 4 as a side dish.

Chilli Apple and Pine Nut Salad

Mix 1 tbsp thai sweet chilli sauce and 1 tbsp lime juice in a small bowl. Quarter and core 2 crisp apples and cut into matchsticks. Toss with chilli lime mixture. Garnish with 2 tbsp toasted pine nuts and 2 tbsp chopped mint leaves. Serves 2 as a side dish to curries or Asian meals.

Perfect Roast Lamb

I love this combination of anchovies and rosemary, which comes from the kitchens of Southern Italy. Don't be put off trying it if you don't like anchovies – they melt away to nothing, adding richness and depth of flavour without a hint of fishiness. Serve with Maple-Roasted Veges and Toss of Peas and Beans (see page 287).

Prep time	15 mins
Cook time	50-60 mins
	+ resting
Serves	8-10

1.3-1.5kg bone-out leg of lamb (carvery roast)

8-10 anchovies, halved lengthwise

16-20 tiny sprigs rosemary, plus extra whole sprigs

1 unpeeled onion, roughly sliced

1 lemon

salt and ground black pepper

Redcurrant Jus
2 tbsp redcurrant jelly

2 cups vegetable stock or water

1 tbsp red wine vinegar

2 tbsp port or red wine

1 tbsp cornflour

2 tbsp cold water

salt and ground black pepper

Use a sharp, thin-bladed knife to make 16-20 narrow, deep cuts all over the lamb. Into each hole stuff half an anchovy fillet (if anchovies are mushy just grab a ½ tsp mound and stuff it deep into each hole). Insert a sprig of rosemary in each hole and chill until ready to cook. Bring back to room temperature for 15 minutes before roasting.

When ready to cook, heat oven to 200°C. Place onion slices in a roasting dish and top with the extra rosemary sprigs and the lamb. Halve the lemon, squeeze the juice over the lamb and put the empty halves in the roasting dish, cut-side down. Season lamb with salt and pepper. Roast until cooked to your liking (about 50-60 minutes for medium-rare). Remove meat from roasting dish, cover with tin foil and a clean teatowel to keep warm, and rest for 10-20 minutes.

While meat rests, make Redcurrant Jus. Drain off and discard fat from the roasting dish, leaving onion, rosemary and lemon. Place the roasting dish over direct heat, add redcurrant jelly, stock or water, vinegar and port or red wine, stir well to release pan brownings and simmer 5-10 minutes. Strain off rosemary, onion and lemon shells and discard. Mix cornflour with cold water and add to the dish, stirring to combine. Simmer over a low heat, stirring, for 1-2 minutes. Season to taste with salt and pepper.

Carve lamb at the table and serve with a jug of Redcurrant Jus.

Planning a special meal to suit the season and the tastes of your family and friends is satisfying on so many levels.

Festive Ham with Cranberry Glaze

Nothing says special occasion quite like a glazed ham. It's the perfect centrepiece for an antipodean Christmas or midsummer feast as it can be eaten at room temperature partnered with a range of salads. Source free-range ham cured by traditional methods if you can – it's better for your tastebuds and your conscience.

Prep time	30 mins
Cook time	1 hour 15 mins
Serves	20-30

1 free-range ham
(about 9kg)

Cranberry Glaze
¾ cup dried cranberries

½ cup cranberry jelly

finely grated zest
of ½ an orange

1 cup orange juice

3 tbsp sugar

1 tsp ground ginger

1 tsp ground allspice

½ tsp five-spice powder

To make the Cranberry Glaze, heat together cranberries, cranberry jelly, orange zest and juice, sugar, ginger, allspice and five-spice powder in a small pot. Bring to a boil, reduce heat to lowest setting, cover and simmer for 15 minutes. Remove from heat and set aside.

When you are ready to cook the ham, preheat oven to 180°C. To remove the skin from the ham, first cut through the skin around the shank end, leaving about 6cm of skin on the shank. Remove the skin by pushing your fingers under it to loosen, leaving a good coating of fat on the ham.

Use a sharp knife to score the surface of the fat into small, even diamonds, taking care not to cut right through to the flesh underneath. Place the ham in a large baking dish and brush liberally all over with warm Cranberry Glaze. Bake until golden and caramelised (about 1 hour), brushing with more glaze 3-4 times during cooking.

Serve hot or at room temperature with any remaining Cranberry Glaze as an accompaniment. The leftovers keep well in the fridge for several days and make great sammies.

Hot Side Dishes

It's handy to have a repertoire of interesting side dishes up your sleeve. Double or triple these recipes to feed more people. For more sides see pages 160 and 184.

Maple-Roasted Veges

Peel ¼ pumpkin and 2 kumara and cut into chunks. Cut 2 unpeeled red onions into segments. Toss in a large roasting dish with 3 tbsp olive oil, 2 tbsp maple syrup and salt and pepper. Spread out in a single layer. Roast at 220°C until tender and caramelised (about 40 minutes), turning about halfway through. Remove from heat and drizzle with 2 tsp sherry vinegar (optional). Serves 6.

Stir-Fried Broccolini and Peanuts

Drop 450g trimmed broccolini or broccoli florets, stems peeled if desired, into lightly salted boiling water and cook for 4 minutes. Drain, cool under cold water and drain again. Heat 2 tbsp neutral oil in a wok or frypan and sizzle 1 crushed clove garlic and 2 finely chopped chillies for a few seconds. Add broccolini or broccoli, 2 tbsp fish sauce, 2 tbsp rice vinegar, 2 tsp sugar and 2 tsp light soy sauce and toss over medium heat for 2-3 minutes. Mix in ½ cup toasted peanuts and serve. Serves 4.

Toss of Peas and Beans

Plunge 300g trimmed green beans into a large pot of boiling water and simmer 3 minutes. Add 300g snow peas and 500g shelled or frozen green peas and bring back to a boil. Remove from heat, drain, cool under cold water and drain again. When ready to serve, heat 2 tbsp olive oil and the finely grated zest of 1 lemon in a frypan or wok. Add drained vegetables and cook over high heat for 1-2 minutes to warm through. Season to taste with salt and pepper. Serves 8-10.

Chilli Ginger Brussels Sprouts

Trim and halve 400g brussels sprouts, drop into a pot of boiling water and simmer 2 minutes. Drain, cool under cold water and drain again. Heat 2 tbsp neutral oil and 1 tsp sesame oil in a frypan and fry 1-2 finely chopped chillies for a few seconds. Add brussels sprouts and 2 tsp sugar and stir-fry over high heat until starting to caramelise (about 5 minutes). Stir in 2 crushed cloves garlic and 1 tbsp coarsely grated fresh ginger, then 2 tbsp rice vinegar and 1 tbsp fish sauce. Serves 4.

Christmas Duck with Allspice Beets

With quality ingredients such as plump duck legs it's very simple to pull together a glamorous dish like this festive platter. This sweet, spicy recipe also works well with chicken legs and the Allspice Beets are a fabulous side dish with any roast.

Prep time	15 mins
Cook time	85-90 mins
Serves	8

8 duck leg quarters

2 tbsp rice vinegar

2 cups pineapple juice

salt and ground black pepper

Allspice Beets
1.5kg beetroot, peeled and cut into 1-1.5cm dice, or a mix of beetroots and carrots, peeled and cut into rounds

¼ cup olive oil

2 tbsp maple syrup

finely grated zest and juice of 1 orange

½ tsp ground allspice

salt and ground black pepper

To serve
¼ cup roughly chopped toasted hazelnuts (see page 78)

mint leaves

To prepare the Allspice Beets, preheat oven to 200°C. Mix together beetroot and carrots, if using, olive oil, maple syrup, orange zest and juice, allspice and salt and pepper to taste. Spread out in a single layer in a large roasting dish. Bake until tender (about 45 minutes). Serve hot or at room temperature. Allspice Beets can be cooked ahead of time and reheated, or put in the oven to cook while the duck is in its second stage of cooking.

To cook the duck, preheat oven to 220°C. Place duck pieces skin side up in a very large roasting dish. Bake for 45 minutes. Remove from oven, drain off fat and discard.

Pour rice vinegar and pineapple juice over the duck and season with salt and pepper. Reduce oven to 200°C and bake until golden and very tender (about 40-45 minutes). Lift duck out of dish and discard cooking liquids (or reduce to a jus if desired).

To serve, place Allspice Beets on a large platter and arrange duck on top. Sprinkle with toasted hazelnuts and mint leaves.

Potatoes on the Side

Potatoes are my all-time favourite starch – it must be the Irish in my husband. I love the way you can make them creamy or crispy and they have a fabulous chameleon quality, taking on so many different flavours with ease.

Spiced Roast Potatoes

Peel about 2.2kg floury potatoes and cut into 2cm chunks. Divide between 2 roasting dishes. Roughly grind 4 tsp cumin seeds and 4 tsp coriander seeds in a spice grinder or mortar and pestle, then add 2 tsp turmeric, 2 tsp ground ginger, 2 tsp salt, 1 tsp ground black pepper and a large pinch of cayenne. Mix into ½ cup neutral oil and then mix through potatoes to coat evenly. Bake at 200°C until crispy and golden (about 45-50 minutes). Serves 8-10.

Garlicky Potato Gratin

Peel and thinly slice about 1.2kg floury potatoes. Layer in a large, buttered baking dish, seasoning with salt and pepper between layers. Mix 3 crushed cloves garlic with 3 cups milk and ½ tsp grated nutmeg. Pour over potatoes, dot with butter, cover and microwave 10 minutes, then uncover and bake at 200°C until golden and tender (about 45-50 minutes). If you don't have a microwave, bake about 1¼ hours. Serves 6.

Fennel and Rosemary Roast Potatoes

Scrub about 1.2kg small potatoes and score a criss-cross pattern on either side. Place in a roasting dish and toss through 2 tbsp olive oil, 1 tsp chopped fennel seeds, 1 tsp rosemary leaves, the finely grated zest of 1 lemon and salt and pepper. Roast at 200°C, turning after 20 minutes, until golden and cooked through (about 45 minutes total). Serves 6.

Olive Oil Mash

Peel about 1.2kg floury potatoes and cut into evenly sized pieces. Place in a large pot with 3 peeled cloves garlic and cover with cold water. Bring to a boil and cook until tender. Drain then mash or pass through a ricer until light and fluffy. Stir in 4 tbsp olive oil, 1 tbsp rice vinegar, 2 tbsp chopped basil, 2 tbsp chopped mint and salt and pepper to taste. Serve hot with a splash of boutique extra virgin olive oil over the top. Serves 6, but I make extra so I can fry some up for breakfast the next day.

Strawberry Limoncello Tiramisu

Limoncello is a Mediterranean lemon liqueur that gives this light summer dessert an intense citrus flavour that prevents it from becoming too sweet. It can be made up to two days in advance and stored in the fridge until needed.

Prep time	30 mins
	+ chilling
Serves	8-10

2 punnets strawberries
or 10 green or yellow kiwifruit

300-350g sponge cake

Limoncello Mousse
3 tsp gelatine

3 tbsp cold water

½ cup boiling water

1 cup caster sugar

⅓ cup lemon juice

½ cup limoncello or water

400g mascarpone

finely grated zest of 1 lemon

Lemon Syrup
¾ cup sugar

¾ cup water

¼ cup lemon juice

¼ cup limoncello or water

To garnish
2 tbsp chopped pistachios

Hull strawberries or peel kiwifruit. Slice thinly and set aside. Cut sponge cake into 3cm chunks.

To make Limoncello Mousse, mix gelatine with cold water to swell, then add boiling water and stir until fully dissolved (or microwave for 30 seconds then stir). Place mixture in the bowl of an electric beater with the sugar, lemon juice and limoncello or water. Beat with whisk attachment until very fluffy and thick (about 15 minutes). Beat in the mascarpone and lemon zest until fully incorporated.

To make Lemon Syrup, heat sugar and water, stirring until sugar dissolves. Remove from heat and add lemon juice and limoncello or water. Tip into a large, shallow tray or baking dish.

Quickly dunk a third of the sponge pieces into Lemon Syrup to wet each side and arrange them in a single layer in the bottom of a 12 cup capacity glass serving bowl. Pour a third of the Limoncello Mousse over the top. Cover with half the strawberries or kiwifruit, then another layer of the dunked sponge pieces. Top with another third of the Limoncello Mousse, then the rest of the fruit and the last third of the dunked sponge. Pour any leftover Lemon Syrup over the sponge layer, then top with the remaining Limoncello Mousse.

Cover and chill for at least 1 hour or up to 48 hours. Garnish with chopped pistachios to serve.

We all look forward to that little moment of sweet indulgence that makes us feel truly spoilt.

Raspberry Jelly Creams

This is a fancy way of tarting up simple ingredients for a special occasion. Serve with or without Brandy Snaps – if you do make Brandy Snaps, remember they respond badly to humidity so are best made on a dry day. Any leftover Brandy Snap mixture can be stored in the fridge for up to 3 weeks.

Prep time   15 mins
Cook time   6 mins
Serves   8-10

2 packets raspberry jelly crystals

2 cups boiling water

1¾ cups cold water

500g frozen or fresh raspberries and/or blueberries

Vanilla Topping
2 cups crème fraiche or greek yoghurt

3 tbsp icing sugar

1 tsp vanilla extract

a pinch of ground cloves

Brandy Snaps
3 tbsp golden syrup

80g butter

⅓ cup soft brown sugar

½ cup flour

2 tsp ground ginger

a pinch of salt

Mix jelly crystals with boiling water to dissolve. Stir in cold water. Divide berries between 8-10 serving glasses and pour jelly over the top. Chill until set (about 30 minutes if berries are frozen or longer if they are fresh). The jellies can be stored covered in the fridge for up to 48 hours until ready to serve.

To make the Vanilla Topping, mix the crème fraiche or yoghurt with the icing sugar, vanilla and cloves. Store covered in the fridge for up to 48 hours until ready to serve.

To make the Brandy Snaps, preheat oven to 180°C and line 2 oven trays with baking paper. Stir the golden syrup, butter and sugar over a medium heat until melted. Add the flour, ginger and salt and stir to combine. Drop small spoonfuls onto prepared trays, allowing plenty of room for them to spread and working in batches so as not to overcrowd the trays.

Bake until golden brown and lacy (about 6 minutes). Remove from the oven and allow to cool flat on trays. When cool and crisp, store in an airtight container.

When you are ready to serve, spoon Vanilla Topping over the set jellies and garnish with Brandy Snaps.

Triple-Chocolate Bombe

Layers of Chocolate Meringue are combined with a rich Chocolate Mousse and topped with Chocolate Ganache to create this spectacular frozen dessert, which is much easier to make than its glamorous appearance might suggest.

Prep time	40 mins
	+ chilling
Cook time	1¼ hours
Serves	20

Chocolate Meringue
5 egg whites

¾ cup sugar

½ cup cocoa

1¾ cups icing sugar

Chocolate Mousse
450g dark chocolate, roughly chopped

3½ cups cream

8 egg whites

1 tsp vanilla extract

Chocolate Ganache
150g dark chocolate, roughly chopped

150ml cream

To serve
fresh raspberries

To make Chocolate Meringue, preheat oven to 150°C. Line 2-3 baking trays with baking paper and mark baking paper with a total of 3 rectangles, each measuring 28cm x 12cm. Whisk egg whites to soft peaks. Beat in sugar a little at a time until the meringue holds stiff peaks. Sift together cocoa and icing sugar and gently fold into meringue. Divide mixture between the 3 rectangles and spread evenly to fit the marked shapes. Bake for 1¼ hours or until meringue is crisp and dry. Allow to cool.

To make Chocolate Mousse, melt chocolate with 1½ cups cream over a gentle heat or in microwave. Stir until completely smooth, then cool. Whisk egg whites until stiff but not dry. In another bowl whisk remaining cream with vanilla to firm peaks. Fold a third of the egg white into the cooled chocolate mixture to lighten the mixture, then gently fold in remaining egg white and cream. Chill until quite firm (2-3 hours or overnight).

To assemble, place a layer of meringue on a serving dish and spread with a 1cm layer of mousse. Cover with further layers of meringue, then mousse, then meringue, pressing meringue into mousse to sandwich firmly. (If the mousse becomes too soft to work with, refrigerate between stages.) Spread mousse all over the finished cake. Cover and freeze overnight or up to 3 weeks.

To make Chocolate Ganache, heat chocolate and cream over a low heat until melted. Whisk until glossy. Allow to cool.

About half an hour before serving, remove bombe from freezer, swirl cooled ganache over the top and sides, and top with raspberries. Allow to soften slightly (about 10-15 minutes) before slicing thinly to serve.

Traditions anchor us and give us a collective
sense of belonging to a place, a culture, a family.
Food is the conduit that brings us all together.

Festive Fruit Mince Tart

If possible, make the filling for this tart well in advance – the longer it sits the more complex its flavours become. This pastry recipe makes enough for two large tarts. You could use the other half to make small Christmas mince tarts – press pastry into muffin tins, fill with fruit mince and top each with a pastry star.

Prep time	20 mins
	+ macerating
	+ chilling
Cook time	45 mins
Makes	1 large tart

Sweet Shortcrust Pastry

360g butter, softened

¾ cup sugar

1 egg

3⅓ cups flour

a pinch of salt

Christmas Fruit Mince

300g currants

150g good-quality raisins, chopped

150g cranberries

3 apples, peeled and grated

1 packed cup soft brown sugar

½ tsp ground cloves

1 tsp ground allspice

finely grated zest
and juice of 1 lemon

½ cup brandy

¾ cup hazelnuts or pine nuts, toasted and chopped

Make the Christmas Fruit Mince at least 24 hours ahead. Place all the ingredients except the nuts in a basin and store in the fridge until required (it will keep for months).

To make Sweet Shortcrust Pastry, beat butter and sugar until fluffy and creamy. Add egg and beat to combine. Add flour and salt and mix until just combined. Turn out onto a lightly floured board (it will be quite soft) and use floured hands to shape into 2 portions. Wrap separately in waxed paper and put half in the freezer for another day. Chill the remaining half for at least 30 minutes before using to make the Festive Fruit Mince Tart.

When ready to cook the tart, preheat oven to 160°C and line the base of a shallow 30cm pie dish with baking paper. Remove the Sweet Shortcrust Pastry from the fridge and roll out thinly to about 40cm in diameter on a second piece of baking paper, sprinkling with a little flour if needed to prevent sticking. Flip into the pie dish then press firmly into the base and sides of the pie dish. Remove the baking paper. Trim excess pastry and reserve scraps for decorations.

Remove Christmas Fruit Mince from the fridge and stir in the hazelnuts or pine nuts. Fill pastry case with Christmas Fruit Mince. Cut stars from the pastry scraps and arrange on top of the tart. Bake until golden (about 45 minutes). Serve warm. Any leftover tart will keep in the fridge for several days.

Christmas Snowballs

With their tangy cherry filling, these buttery, shortbread-like mouthfuls are a regular part of my Christmas baking repertoire. One is never enough, so it's lucky that this recipe, which comes from the family files of my friend Jennifer, is easy to double or triple. You can also use chocolate or other dried fruit in the filling.

Prep time	15 mins
	+ chilling
Cook time	30 mins
Makes	30-36 balls

225g butter,
softened but not melted

½ cup icing sugar,
plus extra for dusting

1 tsp vanilla extract

1¾-2 cups flour

½ cup ground walnuts

30-36 dried cherries

Place butter, icing sugar and vanilla in a mixing bowl or electric mixer and beat until light and fluffy (about 5 minutes). Add 1¾ cups flour and ground walnuts and stir until the mixture comes together into a manageable dough that will hold its shape when rolled into a ball. If mixture is very sticky, add a little more flour. Chill dough until firm enough to handle (about 20-30 minutes).

Preheat oven to 145°C and line 1-2 baking trays with baking paper. Wrap 1 heaped tsp of the mixture around each dried cherry and roll into a ball. Bake in the oven until firm but not browned (about 30 minutes).

When cool, roll in icing sugar and store in an airtight tin for up to 2 weeks or freeze until needed. To serve, place each Christmas Snowball in a colourful paper case.

Christmas Banquet on the Lawn

An antipodean Christmas is the perfect excuse to indulge in a profusion of summer produce, enjoyed at a table laid in the shade of the garden.

🍴

Crab Shooters, page 270

❧

Melon with Mint and Prosciutto, page 272

❧

Christmas Duck with Allspice Beets, page 288

Toss of Peas and Beans, page 287

Maple-Roasted Veges, page 287

❧

Raspberry Jelly Creams, page 295

❧

Christmas Snowballs, page 302

Coffee

Special-Occasion Celebration

My game plan when I'm feeding a crowd is to make generous portions of just a few special dishes. Inviting everyone to help themselves keeps the mood casual.

Champagne with a splash of peach schnapps

❧

Oysters on Brown Bread, page 258

Mussels Florentine, page 262

❧

Sake and Ginger Roasted Salmon, page 278

Festive Ham with Cranberry Glaze, page 284

Asparagus Spears with Parsley Pesto, page 254

Fennel and Rosemary Roast Potatoes, page 290

A leafy green salad

❧

Triple-Chocolate Bombe, page 296

For prep plans, shopping lists and more menus
see annabel-langbein.com

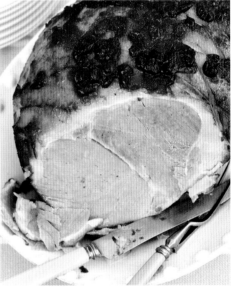

Creating the future

On 11 July 1987 the world's population reached five billion. In 2011 we are already on the roll-over to seven billion. About 250 people are born every minute, 15,000 every hour, 360,000 every day. It's mind-boggling.

It wasn't until I had kids that I started really thinking about the future. Living in New Zealand, where vast tracts of farmland, forest and water separate our cities, you don't get a sense of the pressure being put to bear on the world's resources. But we are one giant, global, interconnected community and the actions of one country or state can quickly affect all of us. We are in this together.

Recently I bought a fancy torch for $5. It was such a bargain I remember thinking, "Wow, shall I get two?" About a month later it stopped working and I discovered that it would cost way more to have it fixed than I had paid for it. Into the bin; buy a new one. It's like a stuck record: new one, new one, new one, consume, consume, consume.

In *Monty Python's Flying Circus*, Mr Creosote, the extremely fat man who is eating to wretched excess at a restaurant, finally takes that fatal mouthful and explodes. It feels as if it's the earth that's about to heave and purge itself of all this "stuff" we so endlessly consume. The trouble is there is nowhere for it to go. Plastic is my bugbear – it seems so convenient and so cheap, but it'll remain on our planet long after we're gone.

It's easy to put your head under a blanket and feel as if it's all doom and gloom. But we need to believe in a great future for our children and their children and for the world to continue to be a beautiful place. We must preserve the marvels of nature and search for harmony, health and happiness. Little things can make a difference. The mantra of reuse, recycle and reduce can bring about change, not just in our own lives but in the broader world we share. There is a pleasing sense of engagement and achievement in being resourceful rather then wasteful, in saving money as well as resources by using less, tuning in to the seasons to shop, and eating fewer barcodes and processed foods.

Future-proofing starts with the next generation – in showing them how to value and care for the world around them and teaching them to discover the pleasures of a simple life.

For more tips on living sustainably see annabel-langbein.com

Glossary

Abbreviations In this book, tsp = teaspoon = 5 ml, tbsp = tablespoon = 15ml, and 1 cup = 250ml. See conversions page for more details.

Al dente Cooked until tender but still firm to the bite; usually refers to pasta and vegetables.

Asian veges Gai lan, bok choy and choy sum are all members of the brassica family. Boil, stir-fry or steam dense varieties such as gai lan for 4-5 minutes and leafy varieties such as bok choy for 1-2 minutes.

Asparagus Snap each stalk as close as you can to its end; it will break naturally just above the tough part. You can then trim the ends neatly before cooking, which takes just 3 minutes in boiling water.

Baking blind This means partially cooking an unfilled pastry shell. Line pie dish with pastry, cover with baking paper then weight down with uncooked rice or beans to prevent the pastry from rising or collapsing at the sides while par-cooking. The cooled rice or beans can be stored in an airtight jar for further use. You can buy ceramic beans which do the same job.

Baking soda = bicarbonate of soda, used as a raising agent in baking and fritters.

Beetroots = beets

Blanch To retain vibrant colour and crunch in green vegetables that are to be used in salads, briefly immerse in boiling water then immediately refresh under cold water and drain.

Broad beans = fava beans

Broccoli and broccolini These are interchangeable. I always peel my broccoli stems – it makes the broccoli tender and the kids are much more likely to eat it!

Burghul = bulgur wheat; a parboiled, cracked and dried wheat available at supermarkets and specialty food stores and health stores.

Buttermilk Now available at most supermarkets, buttermilk looks lumpy and slightly curdled but lasts well in the fridge. It helps make baking light and tender. You can create a substitute by mixing 1 cup milk with 1 tbsp lemon juice.

Caramelise During browning of meat or onions the surface takes on a dark golden colour and this gives a depth of flavour. Also describes the process when sugars are melted to form a caramel, without burning.

Caster sugar = superfine sugar

Chickpeas = garbanzo beans

Chillies To prepare chillies, cut off the stalk end and roll the chilli between your hands to dislodge the seeds. Although smaller chillies are generally hotter, size does not determine heat. Taste a tiny piece before adding to a dish. Chipolte chillies are dried smoked jalapeno chillies.

Chocolate I like to use chocolate containing at least 70 percent cocoa solids, which is now widely available at an affordable price. Chocolate should be stored in a cool, dark place, not refrigerated, as it discolours with fluctuations in humidity or temperature. Using good quality cocoa will also make a big difference to the flavour of your baking.

Citrus The very outer layer of citrus skin is known as the zest. It is full of deliciously flavoured oils and I use lots of it in my cooking as it adds flavour without fat. Unless otherwise stated citrus zest is finely grated. Make sure no white pith gets into the zest when grating as this tastes bitter. To make lemon or lime cheeks as a garnish, cut the sides off a lemon or lime instead of cutting into wedges. To segment an orange or grapefruit, remove all the skin and pith and then cut out the flesh between each segment. Some citrus fruits are far juicier than others. As a guide, the finely grated zest of 1 lime = about 1 tsp; the finely grated zest of 1 lemon = about 2 tsp; the finely grated zest of 1 orange = about 1 tbsp; the juice of 1 lime = about 2 tbsp and the juice of 1 lemon = about 4 tbsp or ¼ cup.

Cook time Use as a guide only. Every oven and stove is different and variations in ingredients and even the room temperature on the day can affect cooking times. To help you develop your free-range style, whenever possible I have given visual cues to doneness, with an approximate cook time as a guide.

Cos lettuce = romaine lettuce

Coriander = cilantro

Cornflour = cornstarch

Cream cheese Do not substitute low-fat varieties when making icings. The consistency is not the same and the icing will not hold its thickness.

Crumbs To make your own fresh breadcrumbs, keep crusts or leftover stale bread in the freezer until you have enough to whizz in the food processor or grate. For dried breadcrumbs, spread out on a baking tray and bake at 180°C until crisp. Store dry breadcrumbs in an airtight container. Fresh crumbs can be stored in the freezer. Crunchy panko crumbs are another handy storecupboard staple. To crumb fish or meat before cooking, dust with seasoned flour or rice flour, dip briefly into beaten egg on both sides, shaking off excess, then roll in breadcrumbs.

Cucumber I often use lebanese cucumbers because they have firmer flesh and a better flavour. If you can't find them, substitute one third of a telegraph cucumber for every lebanese cucumber.

Eggplant = aubergine

Eggs If you are unsure of their freshness, place eggs in a bowl of water. If they are very fresh they will lie flat in the bowl. As they age they start to stand up on end due to the airpocket that develops. When they are rotten they float. When separating eggs it's important you don't get any yolks mixed in with the whites as this prevents them from foaming. Break the eggs one at a time over a small bowl, passing the yolk from one half of the shell to the other while the white drips into the bowl. When making meringue, use eggs that are a week or two old, as fresh whites hold together too well to fluff up. Egg whites freeze well; thaw before using. Unbroken egg yolks can be stored in the fridge for 2-3 days covered with a little cold water.

Fennel Refers to florence fennel bulbs rather than wild fennel.

Florets A head of broccoli or cauliflower contains a number of small florets – it will cook more evenly if cut into evenly sized florets.

Flour Plain (standard) unless otherwise specified. High-grade flour or bakers' flour is high in protein, and hence gluten, which makes it a stronger flour that

should be used only in yeast cookery and for rich fruit cakes and puff pastry. It produces tough, rather than tender, cakes and muffins. Rice flour is useful for pan-frying as it gives a crispy finish. It is gluten-free and widely available at supermarkets.

Free range When it makes a material difference to the taste of a dish, for example when poaching an egg, I have specified free-range eggs, chicken and pork porducts. Where it doesn't, such as in baking, the choice is up to you, but I use free range products whenever possible for the sake of the animals.

Fruits Assume medium sized and washed unless otherwise stated.

Garlic Assume peeled unless otherwise stated. If I want a fine paste texture in garlic I generally crush it by placing the peeled cloves on a board with a sprinkling of salt and applying pressure with the flat side of a wide knife. As a guide, 1 large clove of garlic = about 1 tsp crushed garlic.

Ginger Remove the skin from fresh ginger root before grating, mincing or chopping. Young ginger has thin skin, which can be scrubbed or scraped off, but as it matures the skin becomes denser and needs to be peeled. As with salt, you get more volume when ginger is coarsely grated than when it is finely minced. All measurements in this book are finely grated unless otherwise stated. As a guide, a 2cm piece of ginger root will yield about 1 tsp finely grated ginger or 1 tbsp coarsely grated ginger.

Gingernuts = ginger snaps

Gluten-free With more and more people being diagnosed with gluten intolerances, I have identified the gluten-free recipes in this book with their own icon, and some of my favourites are listed on page 13. When products such as soy sauce are used, I assume you have chosen gluten-free brands, which are now widely available. Gluten lurks in surprising places, so always check the labels before using. Where more than one recipe appears on a page, the gluten-free icon may not apply to all recipes.

Golden syrup If you can't get golden syrup, use brown rice syrup or apple syrup.

Grease Rub the surface of a baking dish or pan with oil or butter to prevent food from sticking.

Grill This can either mean to cook on a barbecue grill or under the heated top element of the oven (broil).

Herbs All herbs in this book are freshly picked and washed unless specified as dried herbs. If a recipe calls for 1 tbsp chopped herbs, remove any tough stems and chop the herbs before measuring.

Icing sugar = confectioners sugar

Kaffir lime leaves A couple of leaves will add a wonderfully exotic flavour. They can be used fresh, dried or frozen. Either leave them whole to infuse flavour into a broth or sauce or remove the central ribs and stems and finely chop the leaves. If not available use finely grated lime zest instead.

Kumara This type of sweet potato has a long history of cultivation in New Zealand. Any kind of sweet potato can be substituted.

Lemongrass Use only the white part. Grate or mince or, if using whole, crush lightly before adding to the dish and remove before serving.

Macerate To soak in a flavouring liquid.

Measurements Some people prefer to weigh their ingredients when cooking; others, like me, prefer to scoop ingredients with a cup. In this book I mostly use cup measurements (1 cup = 250ml) but when it's helpful for you to know a metric weight, for example when it's the size of a tin or tub, I have included that too. Most recipes, even baking, are forgiving enough to cope with slight variations in quantities, as long as you stick with one measuring system. To help you cook in a more relaxed, free-range way, get used to judging common weights and amounts so you don't need to measure them each time. For example, pour a teaspoon of salt onto your hand and remember the size and weight of it, or weigh a 25g handful of salad greens, remembering what it looks like so you don't have to weigh it again. If a recipe calls for 2cm dice, I measure the ingredient against the first joint of my index finger. If it calls for 1cm dice, I measure it against the width of my index finger. Once you develop your own cooking style you will instinctively know when and how to adapt recipes to suit your taste.

Oils Neutral oil refers to flavourless oil such as rice bran or grapeseed. Use cold-pressed oils when possible. When a recipe calls for olive oil, use commercial extra virgin olive oil; when it calls for boutique extra virgin olive oil in dressings or for finishing a dish, this is the time to get out that special bottle. Extra light olive oil is mildly flavoured and can be used for baking or frying. Sesame oil is strongly flavoured, has a low burn point and should be used sparingly.

Onions Assume medium sized and peeled unless otherwise stated. 1 medium onion = about 130g.

Peppers Also known as capsicums or bell peppers. Green peppers are unripe red peppers. To prepare peppers, cut in half and remove the seeds and cores then cut away and discard the white pith. To roast peppers, bake in a 250°C oven until skins are starting to blacken (about 20 minutes). Cover until cool, then peel off skins and discard seeds.

Pinch The amount that can be held between finger and thumb; about an eighth of a teaspoon.

Pomegranate molasses Such a useful, inexpensive ingredient. Widely available at supermarkets, delicatessens and speciality food stores.

Prawns I like to keep a bag of frozen prawn tails in the freezer to defrost for an instant meal. I prefer Australian prawns where possible.

Preheat To heat oven, pan or grill to temperature before beginning to cook. Always allow oven to reach recommended temperature before baking.

Prep time These are approximate so use as a guide only. Includes any time spent actively preparing the dish, including browning and stirring.

Rice This is my foolproof way of cooking rice. For every cup of white rice add 1½ cups cold water and ½ tsp salt. Bring to the boil, stir and cover. Reduce heat to its lowest setting and cook for 12 minutes. Remove from heat and stand for another 12 minutes without lifting the lid. Fluff and serve.

Rocket = arugula

Sear Cook meat over a high heat in a pan to caramelise the outside.

Seasonings When a recipe says to season to taste, simply add enough salt and pepper to make it taste right for you. All recipes use freshly ground black pepper unless otherwise specified. One tsp of fine salt makes a dish a lot saltier than 1 tsp coarse salt.

If you change the kind of salt you use you may need to adjust the amount you use as some types of salt are saltier in flavour than others.

Silver beet = swiss chard

Snow peas = mangetout

Spice mixes Having a selection of quality store-bought spice mixes and pastes in your pantry helps make your cooking quick and interesting. I like to have laksa paste, tandoori marinade, red curry paste, green curry paste, cajun spice mix, miso and tamarind.

Stock Using fresh rather than powdered stock makes a huge difference to your cooking, and it's easy to make using fresh chicken carcasses or the leftover carcass from a chicken roast. Simply cover with water, add an onion, a stick of celery and a few peppercorns and simmer for 30 minutes. I'll often save the cooking water when I boil vegetables and use it as vegetable stock in sauces, soups and gravies – it adds flavour and vitamins and it doesn't cost a cent!

Spring onions = green onions or scallions

Substitutions Follow your instincts when substituting ingredients when something is out of season. If asparagus is out of season, use beans; if you have no broccoli, use cauliflower or Asian greens; if you have no spinach use rocket or silver beet; if you have no shallots use a little red onion. The dish will be slightly different, but still good.

Sugar White unless otherwise stipulated.

Sweetened condensed milk Do not substitute evaporated milk and vice versa. Leftover condensed milk keeps covered in the fridge for months.

Tamarillo = tree tomato

Tamarind If you don't have tamarind concentrate, soak 2 tbsp dried tamarind pulp in ½ cup water until soft, then sieve, capturing the liquid to use in the recipe. Makes equivalent of ½ cup tamarind concentrate.

Temperatures Unless otherwise stated, all recipes in this book have been tested using the fanbake (fan forced) function. If you use regular bake you will generally need to increase the temperature by 10°C and the cook time by 10-15 percent. That said, all ovens cook differently. Use cooking times as a guide and check oven-baked items regularly. Always preheat the oven before you start cooking.

Tomatoes Store fresh tomatoes at room temperature and do not refrigerate. Assume medium size unless otherwise stated. The cores of tomatoes are always tough and horrid. Use a sharp knife to cut them out. When a recipe calls for canned tomatoes, assume they are in juice and juice is used as well.

Vanilla extract/essence Natural vanilla is generally known as extract, while artificial vanilla is called essence. Use extract wherever possible.

Vegetables Assume medium sized and washed unless otherwise stated.

Vegetarian In this book I have identified all recipes that are vegetarian, or that offer a vegetarian option, with a carrot icon. Where more than one recipe appears on a page, the vegetarian icon may not apply to all recipes. Always check the label of store-bought pastes and cultured dairy products to make sure they don't contain animal or fish products. If a recipe calls for a minor ingredient that is not vegetarian, simply substitute a vegetarian option – for example if a recipe calls for fish sauce, substitute tamari. All sweet recipes in this book are vegetarian, with the exception of those that contain gelatin, such as the Strawberry Limoncello Tiramisu.

Whipping Recipes often call for eggs or cream to be whipped to a certain consistency. Soft peaks means when the beater is lifted a peak will form, but it droops at the tip. Stiff peaks means the peak will hold its shape when the beater is lifted. Keep cream in the fridge until the last minute before whipping – it whips better without getting grainy. If you over-whip cream, gently mix through more cold runny cream to bring it back to a soft pillow texture. When whipping egg whites, make sure your bowl and whisk are meticulously clean – any oil or grease will prevent the eggs from fluffing.

Yoghurt Use greek yoghurt for dips and spreads as it is thicker. Use plain, unsweetened yoghurt, which is runnier, for sauces and smoothies.

Zucchini = courgette

For more recipes, kitchen know-how, menu prep plans and gardening advice visit annabel-langbein.com

Conversions

Weights

Where conversions do not match exactly, imperial figures have been rounded up or down.

Metric	Imperial
15g	½ oz
20g	¾ oz
30g	1 oz
45g	1½ oz
50g	1¾ oz
60g	2 oz
75g	2½ oz
90g	3 oz
100g	3½ oz
125g	4 oz / ¼ lb
150g	5 oz
175g	6 oz
200g	6½ oz
225g	7 oz
250g	8 oz / ½ lb
275g	9 oz
500g	16 oz / 1 lb
750g	24 oz / 1½ lb
1kg	32 oz / 2 lb

Liquid measures

This book uses the standard 1 tbsp = 3 tsp = 15ml measure common in New Zealand, the UK and the US. Note an Australian tablespoon is slightly larger so 1 tbsp = 4 tsp = 20ml.

Metric	Cups/spoons	Imperial
5ml	1 tsp	1 tsp
15ml	3 tsp / 1 tbsp	3 tsp / 1 tbsp
60ml	4 tbsp / ¼ cup	2 fl oz
125ml	½ cup	4 fl oz
250ml	1 cup	8 fl oz
375ml	1½ cups	12 fl oz
500ml	2 cups	16 fl oz / 1 US pint
750ml	3 cups	24 fl oz
1 litre	4 cups	32 fl oz

Cup measurements

Even when measured in a standard 250ml (8 fl oz) cup, different ingredients weigh different amounts. Here are some of those most commonly used.

	Metric	Imperial
1 cup almonds (whole)	150g	5 oz
1 cup beans or lentils (dry)	200g	6½ oz
1 cup breadcrumbs (dry)	125g	4 oz
1 cup breadcrumbs (fresh)	60g	2 oz
1 cup biscuit crumbs	90g	3 oz
1 cup butter	250g	8 oz
1 cup cheese (grated)	100g	3½ oz
1 cup cocoa	90g	3 oz
1 cup coconut (desiccated)	100g	3½ oz
1 cup flour (plain)	150g	5 oz
1 cup parmesan (grated)	90g	3 oz
1 cup rice (uncooked)	200g	6½ oz
1 cup sugar, brown (packed)	200g	6½ oz
1 cup sugar, icing	150g	5 oz
1 cup sugar, white	225g	7 oz

Oven temperatures

All recipes in this book have been tested using the fanbake (fan forced) function. If you use regular bake you will generally need to increase the temperature by 10°C and the cook time by 10-15 percent. Cooking times are a guide only.

C	F	Gas
140	275	1
150	300	2
160	325	3
180	350	4
190	375	5
200	400	6
220	425	7
230	450	8
240	475	9

Index

aioli, speedy red pepper, 125
allspice beets, 288
anchovy twists, 251

appetisers and snacks
asparagus spears with parsley pesto, 254
baked ricotta and pine nuts, 116
bruschetta toppings, 244
cauliflower broccoli fritters, mango dip, 256
cheese with prosciutto and bread, 254
crudites, curry mayo and balsamic oil, 254
cucumber salad with salmon, 116
mini chicken tortilla cups, 247
mussels florentine, 262
oysters on brown bread, 258
oysters with kilpatrick topping, 261
smoked fish morsels, 248
smoked salmon au naturel, 254
tomatoes stuffed with chevre and mint, 116
apples, chilli apple and pine nut salad, 280

apricots
baked ricotta and apricot cheesecakes, 232
ginger and apricot biscuit slice, 24
asian chilli dressing, 174
asian slaw with sake dressing, 280

asparagus
asparagus spears with parsley pesto, 254
asparagus tarts, 251
asparagus with poached egg, parmesan, 46

aubergines – see eggplants
avocado, green goddess topping, 244

bacon, tomato and bean soup, 87
baked ricotta and apricot cheesecakes, 232
baked ricotta and pine nuts, 116

baking – see biscuits; cakes; desserts; scones

bananas
banana berry smoothie, dairy-free, 18
banana coconut salad, 223

barbecues – see also skewers
barbecue lemon garlic mushrooms, 160
char-grilled red and yellow peppers, 160
barbecued chicken chickpea toss, 174
grilled flank steak, 176
grilled lamb with spring burghul salad, 174
grilled veges with sesame sauce, 160
grilled kumara, 182
help-yourself hot steak sandwiches, 179
lemon garlic mushrooms, 160
mediterranean lamb salad, 173
mediterranean vegetable toss, 160
scallops with lemon caper butter, 160
snapper with black bean sauce, 160
spicy squid and grapefruit salad, 174
sticky chilli ribs, 182
vegetables, 160

beans – see also chickpeas; lentils
lamb and white bean cassoulet, 217
prawn and bean salad, 80
salad of beets, beans and walnuts, 52
smoky jo soup, 89
tomato, bacon and bean soup, 87
toss of peas and beans, 287
white bean and rocket bruschetta, 244
white bean puree, 244

beef
beef pho, 118
grilled flank steak with quick green sauce, 176
help-yourself hot steak sandwiches, 179
indonesian beef rendang, 220
lime and sesame beef stir-fry, 130
the ultimate beef fillet, 199

beetroot
allspice beets, 288
salad of beets, beans and walnuts, 52

berries – see also particular berries
banana berry smoothie, 18
mixed berry salad, 146

biscuits
brandy snaps, 295
chocolate chip cookies, 32
chocolate coconut ice slice, 31
christmas snowballs, 302
ginger and apricot biscuit slice, 24
gingerbread cookies, 40

blue cheese
broccoli, blue cheese and almond tarts, 251
radicchio salad with blue cheese, 280
roasted cauliflower and blue cheese soup, 87
brandy snaps, 295

broccoli and broccolini
broccoli, blue cheese and almond tarts, 251
broccolini cashew toss, 166
cauliflower broccoli fritters, mango dip, 256
stir-fried and peanuts, 287
brussels sprouts, chilli ginger, 287
burghul, spring salad with grilled lamb, 174

cajun fish tacos, 125

cakes
carrot cake for a crowd, 105
lemon coconut cake, 106
olive oil marble cake, 35
one-pot chocolate raspberry cupcakes, 36
spiced fruit loaf, 38

caramel
caramel bread puddings, 231
caramel custard, 231
caramel oranges and kiwifruit, 146
carrot cake for a crowd, 105

cauliflower
cauliflower broccoli fritters, mango dip, 256
crisp cauliflower and cashew salad, 223
roasted cauliflower and blue cheese soup, 87
char-grilled red and yellow peppers, 160

cheese – see particular cheeses
cheesy rocket scones, 20
cherries, christmas snowballs, 302

chicken
barbecued chicken chickpea toss, 174
chicken and prawn gumbo, 90
chicken noodles with asian greens, 62
chicken tonnato, 140
chicken, fennel and olive tagine, 213
ginger chilli sweet and sour chicken, 134
hearty smoked chicken chowder, 102
lemon chicken skewers, yoghurt sauce, 169
mini chicken tortilla cups, 247
mushroom and chicken tom yum, 61
poached, 140
pot-braised chicken with shiitake, 206
quick smoked chicken pasta, 102
roast chicken platter, rocket and lemon, 77
smoked chicken and mustard pie, 102
thai chicken kebabs, 169
tunisian chicken salad, orange dressing, 121
warm chicken liver salad with hazelnuts, 78

chickpeas
barbecued chicken chickpea toss, 174
spiced chickpeas and haloumi, 58

chillies
asian chilli dressing, 174
chilli apple and pine nut salad, 280
chilli ginger brussels sprouts, 287
chilli mint sauce, 208

chocolate
chocolate chip cookies, 32
chocolate coconut ice slice, 31
chocolate coconut icing, 31
chocolate ganache, 296
chocolate meringue, 296
chocolate mousse, 296
olive oil marble cake, 35
one-pot chocolate raspberry cupcakes, 36
triple-chocolate bombe, 296

chorizo
chicken and prawn gumbo, 90
smoky jo soup, 89
christmas duck with allspice beets, 288
christmas fruit mince, 300
christmas snowballs, 302

coconut
banana coconut salad, 223
chocolate coconut ice slice, 31

chocolate coconut icing, 31
coconut ice swirl icecream, 152
coconut icing, 106
coconut tamarind prawns, 218
ginger and apricot biscuit slice, 24
lemon coconut cake, 106

cookies – see biscuits
courgettes – see zucchini
crab shooters, 270

cranberries
cranberry glaze, 284
cranberry mint sauce, 199
cream cheese icing, 105
creamy mushroom risotto, 128
crisp cauliflower and cashew salad, 223
crudites with curry mayo, balsamic oil, 254

cucumbers
cucumber and yoghurt salad, 223
cucumber salad with salmon, 116
pickled, 116, 278

desserts – see also pies; cakes
baked ricotta and apricot cheesecakes, 232
caramel bread puddings, 231
caramel oranges and kiwifruit, 146
coconut ice swirl icecream, 152
ginger créme brûlee with mango, 226
ginger peach parfait, 151
ginger steamed pudding, 236
jaffa ice icecream, 152
limoncello mousse, 292
mixed berry salad, 146
new york cheesecake, 234
peanut butter and jelly icecream, 152
pistachio praline semifreddo, 229
raspberry jelly creams, 295
rocky road ice cream, 152
semifreddo base, 229
strawberries in balsamic, 146
strawberry limoncello tiramisu, 292
triple-chocolate bombe, 296

dips – see sauces, salsas and dips

dressings
asian chilli dressing, 174
basic vinaigrette, 173
curry mayo, 254
ginger sesame, 72
herby dressing, 184
market noodle salad, 62
orange dressing, 121
sake, 280

drinks
bloody mary mix, 270
crab shooters, 270
dairy-free banana berry smoothie, 18
raw energy juice, 18
tamarillo whizz, 18
tutti-frutti smoothie, 18
wine, 224

duck
christmas duck with allspice beets, 288
duck and mango salad, 72
red duck curry, 143
spicy duck bowl, 144

eggplants
grilled veges with sesame sauce, 160
mediterranean vegetable toss, 160
mediterranean lamb salad, 173
spicy stuffed eggplants, 196

eggs
asparagus, poached egg and parmesan, 46
egg mayo and olive sandwich, 46
fresh herb omelette, 50
ham and egg club sandwiches, 23
smoked salmon and egg gratin, 99
soft-poached egg on mushrooms, 46

fennel
fennel and rosemary roast potatoes, 290
fennel salad, 125
festive fruit mince tart, 300
festive ham with cranberry glaze, 284

feta
feta polenta wedges with roast veges, 194
grated zucchini and feta bruschetta, 244
potato and feta picnic pie, 96
tomato, pesto and feta tartlets, 251
tomatoes stuffed with chevre and mint, 116

fish – see also salmon; shellfish
anchovy twists, 251
cajun fish tacos, 125
malaysian fish laksa, 74
pan-fried fish, speedy red pepper aioli, 125
smoked fish morsels, 248
snapper with black bean sauce, 166
spicy squid and grapefruit salad, 174
sumac and sesame fish, fennel salad, 125
tandoori fish kebabs, 169
fragrant basmati rice, 223
fresh fruit tartlets with mascarpone cream, 108
fresh herb omelette, 50

fruit – see also particular fruits
christmas fruit mince, 300
festive fruit mince tart, 300
fresh fruit tartlets, mascarpone cream, 108
spiced fruit loaf, 38

garlicky potato gratin, 290

ginger
ginger and apricot biscuit slice, 24
ginger chilli sweet and sour chicken, 134
ginger créme brûlee with mango, 226
ginger custard, 226
ginger peach parfait, 151
ginger sesame dressing, 72
ginger steamed pudding, 236
gingerbread cookies, 40
grapefruit salad, 174
grated zucchini and feta bruschetta, 244

grilled flank steak with quick green sauce, 176
grilled kumara, 182
grilled lamb with spring burghul salad, 174
grilled veges with sesame sauce, 160
haloumi, spiced chickpeas and haloumi, 58

ham
festive ham with cranberry glaze, 284
ham and egg club sandwiches, 23
smoky jo soup, 89
hazelnuts, toasted, 78
hearty smoked chicken chowder, 102

herbs
fresh herb omelette, 50
fried garnish, 134
growing, 57
herby dressing, 184

icings
chocolate coconut icing, 31
chocolate ganache, 296
coconut icing, 106
cream cheese icing, 105
in the pink frosting, 36
lemon, 24
royal, 40
indonesian beef rendang, 220
in the pink frosting, 36

jaffa ice icecream, 152
japanese-style rice, 122

juices – see drinks

kebabs – see skewers
kiwifruit and caramel oranges, 146

kumara
grilled, 182
kumara, lentils and watercress soup, 87
laksa base, 74

lamb
grilled lamb with spring burghul salad, 174
lamb and white bean cassoulet, 217
mediterranean lamb salad, 173
perfect made-ahead lamb racks, 208
perfect roast lamb, 282

lemons
easy lemon icing, 24
lemon chicken skewers, 169
lemon chive yoghurt, 116
lemon coconut cake, 106
lemon syrup, 292
lentils, kumara and watercress soup, 87
lime and sesame beef stir-fry, 130
limoncello mousse, 292

malaysian fish laksa, 74

mango
dip, 256
duck and mango salad, 72
ginger créme brûlee with mango, 226
maple-roasted veges, 287

marinades
for beef, 199
for lamb, 173, 174, 208
for pork, 182
for salmon, 278
for squid, 174
market noodle salad, 62
mascarpone cream, 108
meatballs, tuscan, 202
mediterranean lamb salad, 173
mediterranean vegetable toss, 160
melon platter with mint and prosciutto, 272
mini chicken tortilla cups, 247
miso-glazed salmon, 122
mixed berry salad, 146

mushrooms
barbecued lemon garlic mushrooms, 160
creamy mushroom risotto, 128
mushroom and chicken tom yum, 61
soft-poached egg on mushrooms, 47
mussels florentine, 262

noodles
beef pho, 118
chicken noodles with asian greens, 62
malaysian fish laksa, 74
market noodle salad, 62
salmon noodle bowl, 62
spicy duck bowl, 144

olive oil marble cake, 35
olive oil mash, 290
one-pot chocolate and raspberry cupcakes, 36

oranges
caramel oranges and kiwifruit, 146
orange dressing, 121
raspberry and orange sauce, 146
sweet orange scones, 20

oysters
oysters on brown bread, 258
oysters with kilpatrick topping, 261

pan-fried fish, speedy red pepper aioli, 125
parsley pesto, 254
passionfruit topping, 234

pasta
pasta with spinach and walnuts, 133
spinach ricotta gnocchi, walnut butter, 192
pronto pasta with pine nuts, tomatoes, 133
quick smoked chicken pasta, 102
roasted vegetable orzo, 184
salmon, capers and rocket, 133

pastry
food-processor pastry, 100
sweet shortcrust, 300
peach ginger parfait, 151
peanut butter and jelly icecream, 152
peas, toss of peas and beans, 287

peppers
char-grilled red and yellow peppers, 160
mediterranean vegetable toss, 160

perfect made-ahead lamb racks, 208
perfect roast lamb, 282
pesto, parsley, 254
pickled cucumber, 278

pies – see also desserts
anchovy twists, 251
asparagus tarts, 251
broccoli, blue cheese and almond tarts, 251
festive fruit mince tart, 300
fresh fruit tartlets, mascarpone cream, 108
potato and feta picnic pie, 96
raspberry jam shortbreads, 108
roasted plum tarts, 108
sensational spinach tart, 100
smoked chicken and mustard pie, 102
strawberry custard tarts, 108
tomato, pesto and feta tartlets, 251
pineapple salsa, 182
pistachio praline semifreddo, 229
plums, roasted plum tarts, 108
polenta, feta wedges with roast veges, 194

pork
slow-baked pork and apricots, 214
sticky chilli ribs with pineapple salsa, 182
tuscan meatballs, 202

potatoes, 290
fennel and rosemary roast potatoes, 290
garlicky potato gratin, 290
olive oil mash, 290
potato and feta picnic pie, 96
spiced roast potatoes, 290

prawns
chicken and prawn gumbo, 90
coconut tamarind prawns, 218
prawn and bean salad, 80
spring prawn salad, 52
pronto pasta with pine nuts and tomatoes, 133

prosciutto
cheese with prosciutto and bread, 254
melon platter with mint and prosciutto, 272
purple wheat salad, 184

quick smoked chicken pasta, 102
quick zucchini fritters, 49
quinoa salad with tomatoes, 184

radicchio salad with blue cheese, 280

raspberries
raspberry and orange sauce, 146
raspberry jam shortbreads, 108
raspberry jelly creams, 295
raw energy juice, 18
red duck curry, 143
redcurrant jus, 282

rice
creamy mushroom risotto, 128
foolproof, 311
fragrant basmati rice, 223
japanese-style rice, 122
thai-style tofu fried rice, 64

rich tomato sauce, 202

ricotta
baked ricotta and apricot cheesecakes, 232
baked ricotta and pine nuts, 116
spinach ricotta gnocchi, walnut butter, 192
roast chicken platter with rocket and lemon, 77
roasted cauliflower and blue cheese soup, 87
roasted plum tarts, 108
roasted vegetable orzo, 184

rocket
cheesy rocket scones, 20
pasta with salmon, 133
roasted chicken platter, 77
white bean and rocket bruschetta, 244
rocky road ice cream, 152
royal icing, 40

sake and ginger roasted salmon, 278

salads
asian slaw with sake dressing, 280
banana coconut salad, 223
barbecued chicken chickpea toss, 174
chilli apple and pine nut salad, 280
crisp cauliflower and cashew salad, 223
cucumber and yoghurt salad, 223
duck and mango salad, 72
fennel salad, 125
grapefruit salad, 174
grilled lamb with spring burghul salad, 174
market noodle salad, 62
mediterranean lamb salad, 173
melon platter with mint and prosciutto, 272
prawn and bean salad, 80
purple wheat salad, 184
quinoa salad with tomatoes, 184
radicchio salad with blue cheese, 280
roasted vegetable orzo, 184
salad of beets, beans and walnuts, 52
spicy squid and grapefruit salad, 174
spring prawn salad, 52
summer salad with hot-smoked salmon, 52
tunisian chicken salad, orange dressing, 121
warm chicken liver salad with hazelnuts, 78

salmon
cold-smoked salmon and cress sandwiches, 23
cucumber salad with salmon, 116
miso-glazed salmon, 122
pasta with salmon, capers and rocket, 133
sake and ginger roasted salmon, 278
salmon noodle bowl, 62
smoked salmon and egg gratin, 99
smoked salmon au naturel, 254
summer salad with hot-smoked salmon, 52

salsas – see sauces, salsas and dips

sandwiches
cold-smoked salmon sandwiches, cress, 23
egg mayo and olive sandwich, 46
ham and egg club, 23
help-yourself hot steak sandwiches, 179
tuna niçoise on turkish flatbread, 23

sauces, salsas and dips – see also marinades
balsamic oil dip, 254
chilli mint sauce, 208
coconut tamarind sauce, 218
cranberry glaze, 284
cranberry mint sauce, 199
green goddess topping, 244
kilpatrick topping, 261
laksa base, 74
lemon caper butter, 164
lemon chive yoghurt, 116
mango dip, 256
miso glaze, 122
parsley pesto, 254
pineapple salsa, 182
pomegranate vinaigrette, 184
quick green sauce, 176
redcurrant jus, 282
rich tomato sauce, 202
sesame sauce, 160
speedy red pepper aioli, 125
spiked yoghurt sauce, 169
tandoori yoghurt, 169
tonnato sauce, 140
walnut butter, 192
white bean puree, 244
white sauce, 99

sauces, sweet
caramel custard, 231
ginger custard, 226
lemon syrup, 292
passionfruit topping, 234
raspberry and orange, 146
vanilla topping, 295

sausages
chicken and prawn gumbo, 90
smoky jo soup, 89
scallops with lemon caper butter, 164

scones
cheesy rocket, 20
sweet orange, 20
sensational spinach tart, 100
sesame sauce, 160

shellfish – see also fish; prawns
crab shooters, 270
mussels florentine, 262
oysters on brown bread, 258
oysters with kilpatrick topping, 261
scallops with lemon caper butter, 164

side dishes
allspice beets, 288
asian slaw with sake dressing, 280
asparagus spears with parsley pesto, 254
banana coconut salad, 223
barbecue lemon garlic mushrooms, 160
broccolini cashew toss, 166
char-grilled red and yellow peppers, 160
chilli apple and pine nut salad, 280
chilli ginger brussels sprouts, 287
creamy mushroom risotto, 128

crisp cauliflower and cashew salad, 223
cucumber and yoghurt salad, 223
fennel and rosemary roast potatoes, 290
feta polenta wedges, 194
fragrant basmati rice, 223
garlicky potato gratin, 290
grated zucchini and feta, 244
grilled kumara, 182
grilled veges with sesame sauce, 160
japanese-style rice, 122
maple-roasted veges, 287
market noodle salad, 62
mediterranean vegetable toss, 160
olive oil mash, 290
pasta with spinach and walnuts, 133
pronto pasta with pine nuts, tomatoes, 133
purple wheat salad, 184
quinoa salad with tomatoes, 184
radicchio salad with blue cheese, 280
roasted vegetable orzo, 184
roast veges, 194
spiced chickpeas and haloumi, 58
spiced roast potatoes, 290
stir-fried broccolini and peanuts, 287
toss of peas and beans, 287
white bean purée, 244

skewers, 169
lemon chicken skewers, yoghurt sauce, 169
tandoori fish kebabs, 169
thai chicken kebabs, 169

slices – see biscuits
slow-baked pork and apricots, 214

smoked chicken and mustard pie, 102
smoked fish cream morsels, 248
smoked salmon and cress sandwiches, 23
smoked salmon and egg gratin, 99
smoked salmon au naturel, 254
smoky jo soup, 89

smoothies – see drinks
snacks – see appetisers
snapper with black bean sauce, 166
soft-poached egg on mushrooms, 46

soups
beef pho, 118
chicken and prawn gumbo, 90
hearty smoked chicken chowder, 102
lentils, kumara and watercress, 87
malaysian fish laksa, 74
mushroom and chicken tom yum, 61
roasted cauliflower and blue cheese, 87
smoky jo, 89
tomato, bacon and bean, 87
speedy red pepper aioli, 125
spiced chickpeas and haloumi, 58
spiced fruit loaf, 38
spiced roast potatoes, 290
spicy duck bowl, 144
spicy filling, 196
spicy squid and grapefruit salad, 174

spicy stuffed eggplants, 196
spiked yoghurt sauce, 169

spinach
pasta with spinach and walnuts, 133
sensational spinach tart, 100
spinach ricotta gnocchi, walnut butter, 192

starters – see appetisers
sticky chilli ribs with pineapple salsa, 182
stir-fried broccolini and peanuts, 287

strawberries
strawberries in balsamic, 146
strawberry custard tarts, 108
strawberry limoncello tiramisu, 292
sumac and sesame fish with fennel salad, 125
summer salad with hot-smoked salmon, 52
sweet orange scones, 20
sweet shortcrust pastry, 300

tacos, cajun fish, 125
tamarillo whizz, 18
tandoori fish kebabs, 169

tarts – see pies
thai chicken kebabs, 169
thai-style tofu fried rice, 64
the ultimate beef fillet, 199
tofu, thai-style tofu fried rice, 64

tomatoes
rich tomato sauce, 202
tomato, bacon and bean soup, 87
tomato, pesto and feta tartlets, 251
tomatoes stuffed with chevre and mint, 116
tonnato sauce, 140
toss of peas and beans, 287
triple-chocolate bombe, 296

tuna
tonnato sauce, 140
tuna niçoise on turkish flatbread, 23
tunisian chicken salad, orange dressing, 121
tuscan meatballs, 202

vanilla topping, 295

vegetables – see also particular vegetables
barbecued, 160
crudites with curry mayo, balsamic oil, 254
maple-roasted veges, 287
roast veges, 194
roasted vegetable orzo, 184

walnuts
pasta with spinach and walnuts, 133
salad of beets, beans and walnuts, 52
walnut butter, 192
warm chicken liver salad with hazelnuts, 78
watercress, lentils and kumara soup, 87
white bean and rocket bruschetta, 244
white bean puree, 244
white sauce, 99

zucchini
grated zucchini and feta bruschetta, 244
quick zucchini fritters, 49

index

317

Thank you

Our home in the city is like Grand Central Station – a buzzing hub of creative energy, which I love. People come in to help with recipe testing in my kitchen or with publishing my books and producing my website, videos and television series. We often invite clients for drinks or a simple meal on the deck, and once a week the team gathers around a big table for lunch – soup, salad or some kind of savoury tart that's usually a work in progress on the recipe-development front.

At the weekend the house becomes our own again, although it's often filled with the bustle of teenagers baking, or the sounds and smells of a meal being whipped up for friends who've popped in unannounced. There's never a dull moment in the city, and it's this buzz I have tried to capture in this book.

The journey of creating this book has involved a number of very talented people. My special thanks go to the wonderful Melissa Bulkeley, who not only designed this book and managed its production, but also took lots of the photographs, and still found time to bring us homemade cupcakes for morning tea. Also to my editor Jane Binsley – apart from being incredibly good at your job, you make it such fun. How you manage to come to work each day full of vivacious energy, having already organised three small children (who all star in this book) is a wonder to us all!

Working with a team of talented, committed and fun people is a blast and the sense of collaboration and energy is something I truly value. Thanks to our media team led by Susan Warren – Angela, Lisa, Theresa, Vicky and Wendy – it is a pleasure to work with you all. Thank you to photographers Manja Wachsmuth, Aaron McLean, Nick Tresidder and Emma Bass for the wonderful images, and behind the scenes Lesley, Meg, Jo, and all the recipe testers, proofreaders and other helpers. Thanks to NZ Life & Leisure magazine, where some of the recipes first appeared, and to French Country Collections, Corso De' Fiori and Living & Giving for props.

Special thanks to my lovely friends, whose friendship and support add so much to my life, and last but not least to my fabulous family – Ted, Sean and Rose. I wouldn't want to do it without you.

AN ANNABEL LANGBEIN BOOK annabel-langbein.com

First published in 2011 by Annabel Langbein Media Ltd
PO Box 99068, Newmarket, Auckland 1149, New Zealand
First reprint 2011

WORDS, FOOD AND STYLING Annabel Langbein
DESIGN Melissa Bulkeley
EDITOR Jane Binsley

© Recipes and text copyright Annabel Langbein 2011
© Design and layout copyright Annabel Langbein Media 2011
© Photography copyright Annabel Langbein Media 2011, except where listed below.

Thank you to the following photographers, who helped make this book so beautiful, and to NZ Life & Leisure magazine.

© Emma Bass: front cover, back cover (below left), page 113, 136, 157, 175 (middle left, right), 185 (right), 203 (right).

© Manja Wachsmuth: back cover (top left, top right), front and back double page endpapers, page 7, 8, 14, 15, 16, 25, 30, 33 (top right), 37 (top right), 41 (top right, below left), 42, 43, 44, 47 (top left, right), 60 (top right), 63 (below left), 67 (top left), 73 (below right), 75, 76 (below right, top right), 79, 86 (left, middle right, below right), 88, 91, 98 (left, top right), 101, 103 (top left, below left), 104, 109 (right), 110 (middle), 112, 119, 120, 124 (top right, below right), 127 (top left, top right, below middle), 131, 135, 138 (top left, below right), 141 (left), 142, 145, 147 (middle left, right), 154 (middle), 155 (top, middle), 161 (top left), 181, 185 (top left), 186 (top, below), 188, 189, 195, 197, 203 (top left), 204 (top left, top right, below middle), 207, 209, 210, 211, 212, 216 (top right), 219, 221 (right), 222 (left), 225 (top left, right), 227, 230 (top, below left), 235 (top left), 237, 238 (top, middle), 239, 245 (middle, below left), 249, 255 (middle left, right), 257, 259, 260, 266, 267, 268, 271, 273, 274 (top right), 276-277, 279, 281 (middle left, right), 283 (below left), 286 (top, middle, below right), 289, 291 (middle left, below left, right), 293, 294 (left, top right), 297, 298-299, 301, 303, 304, 305 (top, below), 319.

© Aaron McLean: front and back single page endpapers, page 1, 2-3, 4, 34, 47 (below left), 48, 51, 53 (below left), 59, 60 (top left), 63 (top left, middle left, right), 67 (below left, below middle, top right, middle right), 69, 70, 73 (top left, top right, below left), 76 (top left), 81, 97, 103 (middle left, right), 107, 110 (below), 111 (top, middle), 117 (right), 123, 124 (middle right), 127 (below right), 129 (below left), 132 (left, top right), 161 (middle left, right), 165, 167, 168 (top, middle, below right), 172, 175 (top left, below left), 177, 187, 190, 193, 203 (below left), 204 (below right), 215, 216 (below right), 222 (top, middle, below right), 225 (below left), 228, 230 (top right), 233, 235 (below right), 238 (below), 240, 241, 242, 245 (top left, right), 246, 263, 274 (top left, middle right), 281 (top, below left), 283 (below right), 285, 286 (left), 305 (middle), 320.

© Nick Tresidder: page 53 (top left), 109 (top left, below left), 111 (below), 129 (right), 132 (middle right, below right), 255 (below left), 274 (below right), 283 (top right), 291 (top left), 310 (top middle, top right, middle left, middle right, below left and below middle).

All rights reserved. No part of this book may be reproduced in any form, except for brief reviews, without the written permission of the publisher. The right of Annabel Langbein to be identified as the author of this work has been asserted by her in accordance with the Copyright Act, 1994.

ISBN 978-0-9582668-5-7
Produced by Phoenix Offset. Printed in China

Perhaps better known as The Free Range Cook following the international success of her television series and cookbook of that name, Annabel Langbein is recognised as one of New Zealand's most creative culinary figures. Over a career spanning more than two decades she has self-published numerous cookbooks, which have been translated into multiple languages, won a number of international awards, and sold close to two million copies throughout Europe, North America and Australasia.

Annabel divides her time between her home in Auckland, where this book is set, and her family's rustic cabin beside Lake Wanaka, where her television series was filmed. She grows much of her family's fresh produce and draws on her gardens as a source of inspiration for inventive dishes that require very little effort. She is largely a self-taught cook but has attended courses at the Culinary Institute of America in upstate New York and studied horticulture at Lincoln University in New Zealand.

To find out more visit her website at annabel-langbein.com, read her blog at blog.annabel-langbein.com, or follow her on Facebook and Twitter.